Hogan's Boy
A journey in golf

What PGA champions
are saying about...

Hogan's Boy
A journey in golf

John Mahaffey first appeared on my radar by almost stealing one from me at the Tournament of Champions in 1974, when I was playing my best golf. Don't miss this story about John's life in golf, from being a ten-time PGA winner—including a major and a Ryder Cup team—to making the sometimes tortured transition from winding down a playing career to excelling as a golf broadcaster. This book is entertaining, compelling, and honest, and you'll especially enjoy learning about his unique relationship with "The Hawk," Ben Hogan.

Johnny Miller, Professional golfer
25 PGA Tour wins, 2 majors
World Golf Hall of Fame, NBC Lead Golf Analyst

In the final round of the 1970 US Open at Hazeltine, I played with this scrawny amateur from Kerrville, Texas. After I taught him how to hit a fade, he thanked me by almost beating me at the Danny Thomas in Memphis in '72—and he did beat me at the '79 Bob Hope. After that first round together, I predicted John Mahaffey was going to make his mark on golf, but I didn't know that almost a half-century later, I would be reading his excellent autobiography. You'll love the stories of his life in golf, from amateur to PGA professional to TV golf analyst. You'll love reading how John earned the moniker, "Hogan's Boy," and of course, how my fade lesson helped him win ten professional events, including the 1978 PGA.

Lee Trevino, Professional golfer
29 PGA Tour wins, 29 Champions Tour wins
6 majors, World Golf Hall of Fame

Over the almost 40 years I've known John Mahaffey, we've spent a lot of time and played a lot of golf together. If you love the game of golf, you'll fine John's new autobiography—from scrawny Texas teenager to champion golfer to TV broadcaster—very special. The only way it could have been better is if he let me contribute a special "Zoeller on Mahaffey" chapter, instead of this little blurb. Maybe I'll put that in my next book.

Fuzzy Zoeller, Professional golfer
10 PGA Tour wins, 2 Champions Tour wins
2 PGA majors, 1 Champions Tour major

I, too, was fortunate to have played quite a few rounds of golf with the legendary Ben Hogan. I have always felt that he was misunderstood by a lot of people. I always found him friendly, very approachable, and—if anything—a little shy! John and I were fortunate to have played at such a wonderful time in the game, giving us an almost endless number of stories and recollections of some of the true legends. I enjoyed Hogan's Boy *and I am sure you will, too!*

Lanny Wadkins, Professional golfer
21 PGA wins, World Golf Hall of Fame
1 PGA Tour major, 1 Champions Tour win
Lead analyst, Golf Channel Champions Tour

Hogan's Boy

A journey in golf

JOHN MAHAFFEY

with John Caden

Foreword by Arnold Palmer

SBN
BOOKS

Hogan's Boy

A journey in golf

Published in the United States by SBN Books, a division of Small Business Network, Inc., 503 E. Tuscaloosa St., Florence, AL 35630.

This book is available at special discounts for bulk purchases, for sales promotions, or for corporate use. Special editions, including personalized covers or books with corporate logos, can be created in large quantities for special needs. For more information, contact Davonna Blasingame at 256.760.8402 or email dblas@sbnbooks.com.

For speeches, appearances, and outings with John Mahaffey, contact Elizabeth at HogansBoy@comcast.net.

Publisher's Cataloging-in-Publication
(Provided by Quality Books, Inc.)

Mahaffey, John.
Hogan's boy ; a journey in golf / John Mahaffey ; foreword by Arnold Palmer.
pages cm
Includes index.
ISBN 978-0-6159928-4-6
eISBN 978-0-6159964-2-4

1. Mahaffey, John. 2. Hogan, Ben, 1912-1997. 3. Golfers–Biography. I. Title.

GV964.M335A3 2014   796.352092
QBI14-600168

Printed in the United States of America

1 3 5 7 9 10 8 6 4 2

For my father and my mother, whom I miss every day.

It is not the critic who counts;
  not the man who points out how the strong man stumbles,
  or where the doer of deeds could have done them better.

The credit belongs to the man who is actually in the arena,
  whose face is marred by dust and sweat and blood;
  who strives valiantly;
  who errs;
  who comes short again and again,
  because there is no effort without error and shortcoming;
  but who does actually strive to do the deeds;
  who knows great enthusiasms, the great devotions;
  who spends himself in a worthy cause;
  who at the best knows in the end the triumph of high achievement;
  and who at the worst, if he fails, at least fails while daring greatly,
  so that his place shall never be
  with those cold and timid souls
  who neither know victory nor defeat.

—THEODORE ROOSEVELT
SPEECH AT THE SORBONNE
PARIS, FRANCE
APRIL 23, 1910

CONTENTS

*Up to a considerable
point, as I see it, there's nothing
difficult about golf, nothing.*

—Ben Hogan

Acknowledgments

First and foremost, I would like to thank my longtime friend John Caden for reigniting my interest in completing this project. His help and assistance made this book a reality, and his research helped immeasurably throughout the book.

Thanks to Ana Leaird from the PGA Tour, Melanie Hauser from the Golf Writers Association of America, and Todd Jones from the PGA Tour Academy for providing background material and photographs. Thanks also to Leonard Thompson and Lanny Wadkins, two Wake Forest Demon Deacons, for sharing some of their memories.

Special thanks to Davonna Blasingame, Publisher at SBN Books, for all she and her team did to make this book the best it could be.

Most of all, thanks to my wife Elizabeth for her patience and belief in me and most of all for bringing me out of my shell.

*Golf is deceptively simple
and endlessly complicated; it
satisfies the soul and frustrates
the intellect. It is at the same time
rewarding and maddening—and it
is without a doubt the greatest
game mankind has
ever invented.*

—ARNOLD PALMER

FOREWORD

I first laid eyes on John Mahaffey on the first tee at the 1974 Greater Jacksonville Open, when we were paired together. He seemed nervous, as he experienced the commotion of Arnie's Army up close and personal for the first time.

Well, I noticed this scrawny kid from Kerrville, Texas, get over his nerves pretty fast, as he finished second to Hubert Green that Sunday. And even though I didn't care much for being beaten by this upstart, I did appreciate his graciously saying later that his good play was partly due to watching me go about my game that week.

Most people, especially other pros who watch me around the golf course, have noticed I'm always fussing with my clubs—especially the leather grips. I've always used leather grips, and will unwrap and rewrap them in preparation for play. I noticed John was particularly interested in my grips that week, and not long after we played together that first time, he told me I had converted him to using leather grips on his clubs. I took that as a compliment, even though later on I noticed he had abandoned my leather grip system and had gone back to the newer one-piece grips. But that's the great thing about golf: the best way to enjoy the game is to play the way that suits you best.

John played with Rocco Mediate and me the first two days at Oakmont during my last US Open in 1994. I didn't make the cut that week, but as we came to the end of the round on Friday, I hit my second shot to the par-4 18th short of the green and then pitched well past the hole. Even though Rocco and John hit the green in regulation and had birdie putts, they graciously waited to walk on the green until after my pitch.

Oakmont is near my hometown of Latrobe, so Arnie's Army was at full strength and going crazy and I was getting a little emotional. I didn't want to get in the way of my two young playing partners, but I knew when I finished the crowd would go nuts, so I told John and Rocco to finish first. Turns out things got even more out of hand than I thought because, when my 25-foot par putt went in the center of the cup, utter mayhem broke out. John has told me that was one of his great golfing memories, which is saying something since he won the PGA at Oakmont in 1978.

At the 2006 Administaff Small Business Classic (now the Insperity Invitational) at Augusta Pines Golf Club in Spring, Texas, I played my last competitive round on the Champions Tour with Lee Trevino and John. It was another emotional moment in my life. Neither John nor I had any way of knowing that from our first meeting 32 years earlier, he would share so many great memories with me.

During his very successful playing career, John won ten PGA tournaments—including the 1978 PGA Championship—and was a member of the 1979 Ryder Cup as well as the 1978 and 1979 World Cups. And he was a winner on the Champions Tour, too. But as most of us touring pros eventually discover, it's tough making the transition from being successful on the Tour to not being on the Tour. So I'm flattered that John would occasionally seek me out as a sounding board at critical points along his journey. We all need someone to talk to who's been down the road of life—and golf—before, but not everyone is willing to ask for help. Others were there for me, and I was pleased to try to be there for John— and hopefully, I made some contribution.

In 1974 I met a young golfer from Kerrville, Texas, and I predicted he was going to be a winner. Forty years later, John Mahaffey has proved me right. But the thing I'm most proud of is how John has found a way to reinvent himself, from an accomplished PGA touring pro into a successful television golf analyst. Many have tried to make this transition, but not all have succeeded.

I've really enjoyed reliving some of the stories John Mahaffey tells in his new book, and loved reading the ones I didn't know before—and you will, too. There's a lot of history and a lot of honesty here. History and honesty: two things we all love about the game of golf.

—Arnold Palmer

PREFACE

This endeavor began almost a decade ago, with the intention of giving the reader a glimpse into the world of competitive golf. I wanted to use my past to tell a story from the personal perspective of a participant. My objective was to open the window just a crack on an incredibly explosive time in the history of the game of golf and on some of the people who made it happen.

I realize that memories can be fuzzy and we all tend to unintentionally reinvent history at times, but I've tried to stay true to the past as I remember it. As things progressed, it seemed a smörgåsbord of topics surfaced, so I ended up telling a little bit about a lot. The story became autobiographical, historical, philosophical, instructional, inspirational, anecdotal, a little bit silly—and a whole lot of fun to tell.

When I was 13 years old, I had a 12-foot putt to win the PGA Championship. It was a downhill, left-to-right breaker on a lighting-fast green. After surveying the putt from every angle, I stepped up and stroked it into the hole. That day on the putting green at Kerrville Municipal Golf Course, I bagged my 53rd major championship, one shy of the record held by Gary Player.

That was my dream after having just watched Player on television, winning the Masters in 1961. Like most young people who are lucky enough to begin playing golf as juniors, fantasizing about being in contention for major championships was part of my daily routine on the practice green. Ironically, 17 years later, I was fortunate to have such a putt in a real major.

The first time I met Sam Snead, we were paired together at the

Greater Greensboro Classic in 1973. When I introduced myself to him on the first tee, he looked at me and said, "I know who you are, you're Hogan's boy." Almost 30 years later, shortly before Snead's death in 2002, I was visiting his nephew and my good friend, J.C. Snead, at J.C's home in Virginia. During the visit, J.C. suggested that we pay a visit to "Unc," J.C.'s nickname for his famous relative. When we entered Sam's home, J.C. announced that he had brought along a surprise visitor. Sam looked up and beamed, "Well I'll be, it's Hogan's boy."

Hogan's boy.

It's a title I wear like a badge of honor, and this book is the story of how I earned that nickname.

(L-R) Jimmy Demaret, Ben Hogan, Sam Snead and Jackie Burke at the Palm Beach Round Robin, 1950

As I reflect on my life and career in professional golf, it occurs to me that I played during a very special time in the game's history. The legendary players I competed against ranged from the likes of Sam Snead and Ben Hogan, Arnold Palmer and Jack Nicklaus, and on to Tiger Woods and Phil Mickelson, and more. The list of celebrities who supported and played in Tour events during my career reads like a who's who of Hollywood and television stars. Most of those folks are still friends of mine today.

I was fortunate to be in the right place at the right time. In this book I would like to share some of the experiences I've had in a half century of playing amateur golf, collegiate golf, professional tournaments, and pro-ams—as well as being an on-course commentator for Golf Channel. It's been a journey that has surpassed even my loftiest dreams.

Within the pages of this book, I will share stories of the sage advice I've received and the lessons I've learned and applied. I will also introduce you to some real-life characters who have played and are still playing a major role in shaping this game and my life.

I hope you enjoy reading these stories as much as I've enjoyed telling them.

—John Mahaffey

Hogan's Boy
A journey in golf

*I couldn't wait for the sun
to come up the next morning
so that I could get out
on the course again.*

—Ben Hogan

Chapter 1

EARLY YEARS

My incredible adventure began in 1959, the year I first picked up a golf club. Gasoline was 30 cents a gallon, and Coca-Cola was a nickel a bottle. Ben Hogan was still a major factor on the Tour, and Arnold Palmer was charging to victories. Youngsters still rode their bikes to school, and they did not get trophies for just competing—they had to earn them. Winning was the primary objective in any endeavor. One would strive to be exceptional, not just average.

It was a simpler time.

My life got off to a shaky start. When I entered the world on May 9, 1948, I was born premature and was not expected to live. The first month of my life was spent in an incubator before my parents were finally allowed to bring me home. Being about the size of a five-pound sack of sugar, my folks had instructions to feed me at every opportunity to build up my frail body. Since my mother nearly died giving birth to me and was discouraged by our family physician from having any more children, I was destined to be an only child.

After surviving all the newborn issues, I contracted polio at age 4. Fortunately, it was a mild case, but I was bedridden for a while and underwent a rigid physical therapy program to prevent any muscle atrophy. Eventually, I grew out of all my childhood misfortunes, smaller than most my age but with an overwhelming desire to overcome adversity. I loved to compete and grew up in an environment rich in competition.

Kerrville, Texas, is a small town located about an hour northwest of San Antonio. As youngsters in a town of fewer than 10,000 residents in the

3

1950s, my friends and I had vast opportunities to participate in a variety of activities. Kerrville is an absolute diamond in the rough, nestled in the heart of the Texas Hill Country with so much to offer a youngster with an adventurous mind. Parents from all over the world would send their kids to the many camps that dotted the local countryside on the outskirts of town. The climate—with pleasant, breezy nights and low humidity—made central Texas the perfect location for these boys' and girls' camps, many of which were located along the spring-fed local rivers.

The camps offered exposure to a wide variety of activities, including boating, archery, crafts, and more. It was a combination of these attractions—plus the camaraderie—that lured children from many different continents to the Lone Star State each summer. Campers stayed in dormitories, where they learned firsthand the differences and similarities in the customs of fellow boarders and their homelands.

The Guadalupe River flows through the middle of Kerrville, and it provided local youngsters with all sorts of interesting opportunities—including fishing and rafting down some not-so-dangerous rapids that still seemed treacherous to a 10-year-old. This is where my friends and I would spend our summers. We were so lucky that we actually lived there and were able to enjoy all those outdoor benefits without having to pay for them.

> My mother and father were my parents, not my best friends.

In addition to the countryside, there were also the ranches. Some of my parents' friends and a couple of my uncles owned working ranches in the area. This was where I learned a lot about ranching firsthand. In the summers, my cousins and I would spend a couple of weeks at the ranch owned by my Uncle Carl. There we would spend most of the day on horseback, rounding up livestock. When we weren't riding we helped with the never-ending chores around the ranch. We mended fences and cleaned out barns, usually working from sunup to sundown. After the experience of working those summers, the life of a ranch hand lost its appeal. I would prefer to not be on horseback ever again.

Working on the ranch was hard, but it was rewarding. Part of my payment was the ability to use the ranch during hunting and fishing seasons. My dad and I would often go there to hunt dove or to fish in the watering ponds that had been stocked with bass and bream. My father was an excellent marksman and made every shot count. It would normally take him only one shot per dove. On the other hand, I would fill the sky with buckshot and hope for the best. He would look at me and just shake his head. We had such great times together and I really miss them. They were some kind of special.

Family Is Everything

My folks were awesome, and I had the kind of childhood that I wish everyone could have. My mother and father were my parents, not my best friends. They knew that their role was that of teacher. They praised good behavior and punished bad behavior. I respected them for that and learned quickly the difference between right and wrong. We didn't have a lot of money, but we made up for it by doing things as a family with all three of us pitching in.

My dad traveled a great deal of the time on business, and he returned home on the weekends. My mom kept busy taking care of the house, caring for my grandmother, and trying to supervise my activities. There was always so much to do that it was hard to decide what to do next. Mom didn't seem to mind, but I'm sure there were times when my friends and I really tried her patience. I'm sure she was glad when I was old enough to ride my bike. My parents were always there for me, and I have fond memories of growing up in a loving environment.

As I got a little older, my interests drifted toward sports. I played everything available: football, baseball, track, tennis—and my first love, basketball. I would practice basketball for hours, shooting baskets alone in my backyard or in the high school gymnasium. My dad built a plywood backboard for me and nailed it to a tree in the backyard. Then he carefully measured to make sure the basket was set at exactly ten feet high, and fastened it to the board. A lot of work, but he wanted me to have a place to shoot at home, so he made it happen. My dad never had time for sports; he had worked all his life. Dad's own father was taken ill when he was very young, so it seems that Dad was always the breadwinner of his family.

My father was a remarkable man who cared about others and was always there with a helping hand. I trusted and respected him because he was a man of his word. Following his lead, no matter what I did, I always tried to be the best at it. I admired my dad's attitude, as well as his strong belief in God and country. I always hoped that I could follow in his footsteps.

After World War II, my father, John D. Mahaffey, moved from his home in Fort Worth to Kerrville. He never talked about the war, so I was surprised after he passed away when I found the Bronze Star he was awarded for valor. I never knew. He rarely talked about anything negative, always the positive—which is why it seemed natural when he became a deacon in our church.

My dad receiving the Bronze Star during World War II

After retiring from active service as a lieutenant, my dad landed a job as traffic manager with the Kerrville Bus Company. That bus company was an affiliate of Greyhound Bus Lines, but it also operated charter service throughout Texas, Oklahoma, and New Mexico. It had true growth potential, and my dad grew with it. As the years passed, I watched with pride as he moved through the ranks of his company, eventually ending up as president and chairman of the board.

My dad was goal driven and worked hard. He taught me that I could do anything if I was willing to work hard enough. My father had a quiet confidence that was reinforced by his approach to business, which spoke to the adage that a man's word was his bond. He was an honest man of principle and a great role model.

My father was hands-on but fair when it came to discipline. He led by example and emphasized the importance of working to earn something. I was expected to contribute around the house while I was growing up, earning an allowance only if I completed my chores. As I grew older I made extra money at the public golf course by caddying and shagging practice balls (something that I do not miss at all since being a human target in a field of spherical missiles, usually launched by unpredictable swings, is not my idea of fun).

The only physical confrontation that I ever had with my father came on the eve of our first trip to the University of Houston. He and my mother thought that I needed to learn how to tie a tie before I went to college. Up to that point I'd used a clip-on tie with my suit when I went to church. I didn't see the need to acquire this particular skill, and I refused. When an argument ensued, I took a swing at my dad. A second later I was flat on my back, looking up and wondering what had hit me. It was obvious that my father was still capable of using the hand-to-hand combat skills that were part of his Army training. That night I learned to tie a tie.

As a postscript to that story, after a couple of months at school, I called home one evening laughing and my dad asked what was so funny. I told him that of all the people living in the athletic dorm at the University of Houston, it seemed I was the only one who could tie a tie. I was tying ties for

My father during World War II

athletes in every sport, including large football players with huge necks. It was a great way to make friends and acquire some personal security as well.

My mother and father met shortly after he came to Kerrville from Fort Worth. My mother, Dorothy Eloise Wied, had a tough go for quite some time before that day. Her father died when she was young. He was working on a car and had it jacked up so he could get under it. The jack failed and the car crashed to the ground, crushing him.

7

My grandmother, Meta Paul, was faced with a dilemma when her husband died so suddenly. He was the breadwinner for Nana, my mother, her brother Henry, and her sister Thelma—who all lived together in the same house. My grandmother, who was full-blooded German, was a fabulous cook, so she decided to turn her home into a boarding house. In no time, they had all the boarders they could handle. It was hard work but they managed to scrape by. Most of the boarders in my grandmother's house were young Germans, just starting out in adult life. They were energetic and loved living in my grandmother's house so much they would often pitch in with the chores. Most of these early boarders stayed on in Kerrville and remained friends of my mother's throughout her lifetime.

There were a lot of folks of German descent who had settled in the Kerrville area. They had opened a variety of businesses such as restaurants, icehouses, and accounting firms. One of my mother's uncles opened Henke Meat Market. These German Americans were a tight-knit group and would always help each other if necessary. They were also very patriotic. One of our relatives from the Henke side of the family was Admiral Chester W. Nimitz, the Commander of US Naval Forces in the Pacific during World War II, who hailed from nearby Fredericksburg.

Kerrville, Texas, was small-town America as depicted in a Norman Rockwell painting.

In the early 1940s, my mother met and married an officer in the Air Force who promptly shipped out for the Pacific. The bliss of being a young newlywed was shattered the day my mom received a formal letter informing her that her husband, Major Charles Thomas Dozier, had been killed in action in a bombing raid over Nagoya, Japan. He was the navigator on a B-29 that had been shot down with no survivors. Charlie had become the center of her world, a devil-may-care sort of fellow who was always the life of the party. She was devastated. Thank goodness she had so many friends and family to help her through such a difficult time. Even so, it was very hard for her. Charlie is memorialized at the Manila American Cemetery at Fort Bonifacio in the Philippines. He was posthumously awarded the Air Medal and the Purple Heart.

When my mother met my dad, things started to change for the better.

They dated, married, and set up house at 600 Lois St. in Kerrville. It was small-town America as depicted in a Norman Rockwell painting, including the white picket fence. My mother had a wonderful personality and loved to entertain. It was not unusual for the backyard to be filled with people on summer evenings, talking and laughing in the mild Hill Country climate. These occasions didn't happen often enough for my mom, as she adored a party. Although my folks didn't have much money, they had their dreams and were given the opportunity to fulfill them as my dad moved up the ladder with the Kerrville Bus Company.

My mother and father,
John and Eloise Mahaffey

Boy Meets Golf

In late August of 1959, I was formally introduced to the game of golf by a couple of my best childhood friends, Jim Stehling and Scott Parker. I was 11 years old and was immediately fascinated by the game. Over the next few years, hitting golf balls became a passion for me. Like most golfers, I loved the feel of a well-struck shot and the sight of the ball flying toward my target. The challenge was repeating these shots, and just like a compulsive gambler, I was hooked. Golf was, far and away, the most difficult sport for me, but I loved to practice and was resolved to get better.

At the time, neither of my parents played golf, and therefore owned no golf clubs. So with a set of clubs borrowed from my uncle, Henry Wied, I would practice for hours in a field adjacent to the ninth green at the nine-hole municipal golf course in Kerrville. The field was a makeshift practice area consisting of a dirt mound riddled with flint rocks. I carried a file and small hammer in my bag to repair any damage done to a club by the ever-present invisible hazards hidden just below the surface. This game was a lot harder than it had first appeared, but I was determined to get better— although I seemed to be making little progress. In the summertime, I would arrive at the course just after sunup and leave when it got dark. In the morning I would either caddie or shag balls, and then I'd play and practice in the afternoon. That was my daily routine as I was working to find a consistent swing.

At that point, I'd learned the most about golf from the Arredondo family. Tommy Senior was the greens superintendent at Kerrville Municipal and a very good player. His sons Tommy Junior, Ralph, and Joe were also accomplished players and my main competitors early on. These fellows were very eager to teach me some of the basics of competition, usually at my expense. They all had terrific short games, and I learned some of those lessons the hard way as they showed me that imagination around the green was more important than mere technique. It was about scoring, not pretty swings. Through the air, along the ground, bump and run—they had every shot. They were always hard to beat because they were never out of a hole. It was on-the-job training at its best.

Ben Hogan's book became my bible for learning to play golf.

One hot summer afternoon, I was hitting balls in my usual rapid-fire mode when I looked up to see a golf cart coming down the hill toward the practice tee. I recognized the driver as a gentleman who vacationed in the Hill Country every summer to escape the humidity in Houston. Otis Meredith was a renowned lawyer and a member of River Oaks Country Club in Houston. He got out of his golf cart, walked over to me, and introduced himself. He had a small book with him with a golfer's likeness on the cover. Mr. Meredith commented that he had been watching me practice all summer and thought I might benefit from an instructional book written by a friend of his from Fort Worth. He said he admired my work ethic, but it appeared to him that I was getting nowhere, and thought this book might help. I thanked him and began to thumb through the illustrated book: *Five Lessons: The Modern Fundamentals of Golf* by Ben Hogan. It became my bible for learning to play golf. Although I was unaware of it at the time, this also marked the beginning of my relationship with Ben Hogan.

My Introduction to Professional Golf

The first professional golf tournament I ever saw was the Texas Open at Oak Hills Country Club in San Antonio. My Uncle Henry, the one who loaned me his golf clubs when I started playing, was nice enough to take me along with him.

The whole scene amazed me. Up until then the only professional golf I'd ever seen was on our black-and-white television. Much like Billy Crystal's first baseball game, this was the first time I saw a golf tournament in color. The lush fairways and the manicured greens were totally different from the hardscrabble terrain at Kerrville Municipal. The brightly colored outfits worn by the players in contrast with the deep green of the golf course created an image I remember to this day.

We followed Chi Chi Rodriguez, who was playing with Gene Littler. The contrast was incredible. Chi Chi's slashing flamboyance was an incredible contrast to Littler's fluid, almost metronomic swing. This was also the first time I saw Arnold Palmer in person. It was impossible to get very close to him because, as usual, a tremendous gallery surrounded him. Even from a distance, he seemed bigger than life—I was in awe. That experience at Oak Hills made such an impression on me that, right then and there, I decided what I really wanted to be: a touring golf professional. On the way back to Kerrville, I'm sure I drove my uncle crazy babbling on and on about the day.

One of the ironies in this story is that years later, I crossed paths with each of these players. My crude imitation of Chi Chi became a staple of my routine when conducting a golf clinic. Additionally, I was lucky enough to be paired with Gene Littler in the Jeremy Ranch Jr./Sr. Shootout in 1985. Arnold Palmer is the focal point of some of my greatest memories of the game, and I was lucky enough to be in the same group with him at some memorable times late in his career.

> I decided at the Texas Open in 1959 that I really wanted to be a touring golf professional.

Thinking back, I was actually a bit nervous being teamed with Gene Littler when we played at Jeremy Ranch. I'd always had the impression Gene was pretty straitlaced. On the other hand, since I had a tendency to let go with an occasional expletive when I hit a bad shot, I didn't want to upset him with a spontaneous outburst. On the very first hole of our first practice round, however, he laid the sod over a shot and moved the ball about 20 yards. Then, under his breath, he let go with a brief, graphically descriptive statement concerning his displeasure with that particular swing. I smiled and thought to myself, *We're going to be just fine.* We were, too, as we lost the tournament in a playoff with Ben Crenshaw and Miller Barber when they made eagle on the third extra hole.

Besides being the source for my comedy routine, Chi Chi helped me greatly with my bunker game. He was a magician with his "sanwich," and he generously shared his knowledge with me.

When I entered Tivy High School in the fall of 1962, I was involved in almost every sport, including football, basketball, tennis, and golf. During my sophomore year my parents tried to convince me to abandon football, but I was adamant and did not want to quit.

One day our team was playing a game in Del Rio. I was a member of the kickoff team. When we kicked off, as the play moved to the other side of the field, my job was to hold my ground on the opposite side of the field in case the return man reversed field. This day that return man was

High School graduation

6 foot 2, 185 pounds, and fast. I was all of 95 pounds soaking wet. As fate would have it, he did reverse field and ran right over me. I grabbed on to one of his legs, closed my eyes, gritted my teeth, and held on for dear life. He stopped 45 yards later—after he had crossed the goal line—and shook me off of his leg. I opened my eyes to discover that I was looking through the ear hole of my helmet and had a huge divot of grass hanging from my facemask. After the game, my father was waiting for me when I came out of the locker room. He simply said, "Well, that was interesting—so now what do you think?" That was enough football for me.

Although football glory eluded me, I did have a pretty good high school career in basketball, and I actually set a new (but short-lived) school record when I scored 40 points in one game. Unfortunately, no matter how hard I worked to improve my shooting, dribbling, and passing, there was nothing I could do to increase my size. I would always be vertically challenged.

In my junior year, I decided to forgo tennis and concentrate on just basketball and golf. My golf game continued to improve throughout high school. I played on Tivy's four-man team, along with two of the three Arredondo brothers and another friend of mine, Jack Jarrell. I broke par for the first time during my sophomore year.

In the summers, I also participated in many local junior golf tournaments. During one of those events in San Antonio, I met Hal Underwood, a player from Del Rio. Hal was two years older than me and was on his way to the University of Houston. In a few years, that meeting would prove to be fortuitous.

During the 1960s, Arnold Palmer dominated professional golf in the early part of the decade and Jack Nicklaus rose to prominence in the latter part. Of the 40 major championships played during the '60s, Nicklaus won 7 and Arnie won 6. When you throw in Gary Player's 4 majors, you can understand why these guys were referred to as the Big Three.

The other big factor in professional golf during those years was television. Once legendary CBS Sports producer Frank Chirkinian came up with a way for viewers to better follow the action by displaying players' scores relative to par, watching golf on TV became a popular way for folks up north to spend a wintry weekend afternoon. Add in Arnold Palmer's "everyman" charisma and it wasn't long before sponsorships and prize money grew. In fact, prize money grew fivefold—in 1960, the average tournament purse was $32,000, but by the end of the decade, the average purse was $125,000.

Thanks to television, I was able to see golf as part of a bigger picture. I watched tournaments in such exotic places as Hawaii, California, and Florida, and the guys playing on TV quickly became my heroes. I became more and more convinced that what they did was what I wanted to do.

Only bad golfers are lucky.
They're the ones bouncing balls
off trees, curbs, turtles, and cars.
Good golfers have bad luck. When
you hit the ball straight, a funny
bounce is bound to
be unlucky.

—LEE TREVINO

Chapter 2

COLLEGE DAYS

In my senior year of high school, I entered the Texas State Junior Championship. I played my way through the match play bracket and lost the 36-hole championship match on the last hole to a golfer from Midland named Terry Jastrow. Terry would go on to become a producer of golf events for ABC Sports, hold a similar role for Jack Nicklaus Productions, and marry the film actress Anne Archer, a beautiful and very talented lady. Later on in my career I would have the opportunity to work briefly with Terry at ABC, as well as partner with him at the Bing Crosby Pro-Am a couple of times. We had a lot of laughs doing both.

Following a good high school career, and having played well in many junior tournaments, I thought I had the ability to play golf at the college level. However, it seemed I was the only one who felt that way, as I'd not been recruited by anyone. I wrote letters to the coaches at both the University of Texas and Texas Tech, offering to try out for their teams as a walk-on, but neither coach replied. Later on, I would take great delight in going out of my way to ask George Hannon, the UT coach, how things were going whenever we beat them. It was always sweet revenge, especially in the NCAAs. I never had the chance to do the same to the Texas Tech coach, as that team never seemed to make it to the NCAA Championships.

All of this apparent lack of interest was depressing, which is why it was such a shock when, on the very evening I lost that final match to Terry Jastrow, I got a call from Dave Williams—coach of the University of Houston golf team—offering me a partial scholarship to play for the Cougars!

Joining an NCAA Championship Dynasty

To call Houston a powerhouse in college golf would be a gross understatement. When Coach Williams called, the Coogs had won the NCAA championship in nine of the last eleven years, including the last three in a row. In one of the two years they didn't win, they finished second by one shot. Going from not being recruited at all to now having the opportunity to join a golf dynasty quickly ended whatever depression I may have been feeling. I found out later that it was my old friend, Hal Underwood, currently starring for Houston, who brought me onto Coach Williams's radar screen.

The University of Houston is an urban college, and most of the students were commuters. Golf team members were housed in the athletic dorm, which was shared with athletes from all sports. There were 20 players on the Houston freshman team in 1966. At the time, freshmen were not allowed to play varsity sports, but we did play an intense freshman schedule. There were some fine players on our freshman team, including Terry Jastrow, John Grace (who would be runner-up to Jerry Pate in the 1974 US Amateur) and Tom Jenkins (who would have a successful career on both the PGA and Champions Tours).

> My teammates were a source of valuable help in developing my game.

Houston didn't play individual matches but focused on tournaments. Our freshman team played in about 12 such tournaments, and we had to qualify for the team every week. Since there were only 5 guys on the traveling team, this meant 15 guys stayed home each week. I worked very hard during my freshman year so that I would not only get to play each week but also retain my partial scholarship for the next year.

We had some great guys on our team, and I had to really develop my game to keep pace with them. Hogan's book was my bible through high school and continued as my main instruction source while playing golf for the University of Houston. A few of the other guys on the team, such as Doug Olson, had also studied the book. Doug was a member of our 1969 NCAA championship team. He was mesmerized by Hogan's philosophy of golf and had a collection of all his books. We had some lively discussions about our interpretations of what Hogan had written.

My teammates were a source of valuable help in developing my game. When I arrived on campus, I couldn't hit a bunker shot to save my life. Bob Barbarossa, who was taught by Julius Boros, showed me how to hit this shot by taking a wide-open stance and spanking the sand behind the ball. Each day after classes I would go to a nearby municipal course and practice bunker shots. I would take my practice bag full of balls to the bunker at the range and spend hours hitting bunker shots from all kinds of lies. Thanks to Bob's advice and Boros's technique, I became a pretty good bunker player.

Hal Underwood taught me how to tough it out and score on days when I didn't have my best stuff. Hal was team captain and one of the most talented players I've ever known. He is a marvelous teacher who settled in the Houston area after a brief career on the PGA Tour.

For me, John Grace defined fairway wood play. I would watch in awe when he practiced this shot, as I found his method a great way to play fairway wood shots. John would actually take a slight divot on these shots and was as accurate with his woods as most players are with wedges. John would be number one on my list of all-time, top-five fairway wood players, which includes the likes of Deane Beman and Corey Pavin.

The qualification process intensified in my sophomore year. Not only did we all have to qualify for the team each week, but I also had to qualify each year to keep my scholarship. Although this system was brutal, it toughened us and we became better players for it. This may explain why Houston was so tough in big events. Coach Williams was not a golf instructor and didn't pretend to be. His role was to keep the team razor sharp, and his qualification process did just that.

Dave Williams, Univ. of Houston Golf Team Coach (1951–1985)

Coach Williams felt as though the golf team was a fraternity in itself, so we were not allowed to pledge a social fraternity. We did, however, have our own initiation rites—which included getting a buzz haircut and wearing a Wiffle golf ball on top of your head, attached with a red ribbon tied into a bow under the chin. Fortunately, we only had to endure this treatment for the first semester of our freshman year. There were a few other initiation activities, all designed to make you feel part of something special. What made it special was knowing that every player before you had undergone similar harassment. It was, and still is a special honor to be part of that tradition of winning championships.

When we got to the NCAA Championships in my sophomore year, the pressure was really on the Cougars. Houston had won each of the last five championships and we were heavily favored. Although I played pretty well, we ran into a red-hot University of Florida team who edged us by two shots and walked away with the trophy.

As the youngest player on the team, I had to ride back to Houston from Las Cruces, New Mexico, alone in the car with Coach Williams. The fact that I shot in the 60s in the final round no doubt saved me from some of Coach's wrath, but not all of it. It was quite a long drive back, with him driving less than the speed limit and mumbling about no-playing, choking idiots. He had a burning desire to win and would accept nothing less—and I mean nothing. As we drove back to campus, he droned on about how the next year he was going to initiate many new bizarre methods to create golfers who could win. I finally had to turn a deaf ear and go to sleep. I don't think he appreciated it, but enough was enough.

> Summers during my college years were spent playing all the competitive golf I could find.

Summers during my college years were spent playing all the competitive golf I could find. There was an unspoken understanding that we were expected to play summer golf, although the school couldn't finance any of it due to NCAA rules. Financing my participation in these tournaments was a burden on my folks, but somehow my dad managed to make it happen. With their support, I was able to play in a majority of the nationwide amateur events each summer.

In my junior year, Houston really dominated the season. By the time we reached the NCAA Championships, the Cougars had won 14 tournaments and I'd won the individual title in 5 of them, including a stretch of 3 in a row. That year, the national championship was being played at the Broadmoor Golf Club in Colorado. Our main competition was Wake Forest, who had a team that featured a number of future PGA Tour stars such as Leonard Thompson, Joe Inman, and Lanny Wadkins. On the final day, halfway through the round, the wind came up and so did the scores. Bob Barbarossa played great and finished in second place. Our team hung in there and just held off the Demon Deacons by two shots. We regained what we felt was our championship, and I was named first team All American.

In 1970, my senior year found me juggling golf and studies, trying to graduate on time. Academically, I began my college career as a business major. My grades were pretty good, but I was honestly not excited with some of the course material. As part of the business curriculum, we had to take a course in abnormal psychology, taught by a professor who really caught my attention. Some would say that my interest in abnormal psychology explains a lot about me even today. The truth is, I really enjoyed the subject matter and switched my major from business to psychology as a result.

> Some would say that my interest in abnormal psychology explains a lot about me even today.

Although my course load for my last semester was 18 hours, I did find the time to qualify for the 1970 US Open, which was being played at Hazeltine Country Club, in Chaska, Minnesota, just outside of Minneapolis.

My First Major

Although I'd played in a number of prestigious amateur events, the US Open was, far and away, bigger than anything I'd ever been around.

When I arrived at the golf course, it was exciting just to see such stars as Arnold Palmer, Jack Nicklaus, Gary Player, and Tom Weiskopf walking around, let alone to be competing against them. They assigned me a locker close to Orville Moody, who had won the US Open at Champions the preceding year. That morning, as fate would have it, Orville sat down on the bench in front of his locker to change into his golf shoes. I was sitting across from him doing the same, and he glanced over at me and grinned. Then to my surprise he asked, "Gotta game today?" I said no, and he said, "Saddle up, let's go."

To have your first practice round in a US Open with the reigning champion was, in itself, unbelievable, but that was just the beginning of a magical week. Orville hit the ball great and was always in play. I could see how his game was suited to tournaments that required accuracy, like a US Open.

Hazeltine was a relatively new course that had been recently added to US Open venues, and it was hosting the tournament for the first time. The design of the course contained an unusually large number of blind shots. That design feature, along with the fact that the course was not in pristine condition, led to some harsh criticism from many of the contestants. A combination of these conditions, along with the gusty winds that blew all week, had a major impact on the scores. When the dust settled, Tony Jacklin was the only player to finish under par, winning by seven shots over Dave Hill. Tony's experience in managing the ever-changing winds on British courses where he grew up was an obvious factor in his dramatic win. What that win in 1970, Jacklin became the first Englishman to win the US Open since Cyril Walker in 1924 and the last until 2013, when Justin Rose won at Merion.

I had a good tournament, with two strong middle rounds sandwiched between a pair of 77s. My score was good enough to tie for low amateur with Ben Crenshaw. In the final round, I was paired with Lee Trevino and shot a 77 to his 70. My score was disappointing, but following the round, Lee took me aside, congratulated me on tying for low amateur, and asked me if I intended to try to play golf professionally. I said I'd been thinking about it for quite some time and was definitely interested.

Trevino said if I wanted to win on the pro tour, I would need to learn to hit the ball from left to right.

Trevino said that with my game, which consisted entirely of right-to-left shots, I might be able to compete on the PGA Tour. However, he said if I wanted to win, I would need to learn to hit the ball from left to right. Greens on the pro tour were harder and faster, and it would be difficult to keep the ball on the green by just hitting draws, especially with long irons. The higher ball flight of the fade would land softer. Additionally, it is easier to control a tee shot with a fade, which reduces the amount of roll on the ball, often preventing it from running through the fairway and ending up in the rough.

Amazingly, Lee Trevino then proceeded to take me out to the driving range and teach me how to hit a fade. Trevino's explanation made perfect sense, and I adapted to it quickly.

This was my first step in transitioning from being just a good golfer to becoming a player. Trevino showed me how one-dimensional my game was at that time. He opened the door to seeing golf from an entirely different perspective. When your game is one-dimensional, you only have one shot to play. In my case, everything was right to left. Depending on pin locations, only having one shot often would present challenges. It was difficult for me to get the ball close to a pin set on the far right side of a green.

Shotmaking

Learning to expand my array of shots expanded my view of the golf course. When I learned to hit a fade, it opened up the entire left side of the course for me. Pin positions no longer mattered, as I could now approach the hole from either side. Thanks to Lee Trevino, I also learned the importance of putting the ball in position for my next shot. Since I was never going to be a power hitter, it was necessary for me to learn to work the golf ball and become a really good shotmaker.

If a person whose normal shot is a draw wants to become a shotmaker, then he or she needs to learn to hit a fade. Conversely, if a person's normal ball flight is left to right, then he or she also needs to learn to work the ball from right to left.

Lee Trevino's game evolved through trial and error. He experimented with different swings and learned that to hit those shots, your swing path must follow your body lines. You use your body lines to move the golf ball. As a result of what he taught me, I discovered that a simple way to hit a right-to-left shot is to take your normal stance and alignment and then, while keeping the clubface pointing to your target, move your right foot back. This will close your hips and shoulders. Your swing path follows a series of parallel lines created by your feet, hips, and shoulders, so moving your right foot back will bring the club head from inside out, creating the right-to-left flight of the ball. You can experiment with the degree to which you close your stance to learn the amount of right-to-left movement produced. Generally, the more the stance is closed, the more the ball will draw.

To hit a fade, you do the exact opposite: keep the clubface lined to your target, but drop the left foot back a little. This will open your stance and cause the swing path to move along those parallel lines that cross the target line from outside in. This path will result in a shot that moves from left to right. I learned to use my time on the driving range to develop these shots and to learn how they work. I would pick out a target, such as a yardage marker or a flag, and work the ball both ways until I got comfortable with these swings. As I became more and more comfortable, I experimented with stances that were more open, less open, more closed, or less closed. I would try to see how much draw or fade I could generate.

> Some of my fondest memories of practice rounds revolve around creating exaggerated shots over, under, and around obstacles with friends like Tom Watson and Andy North.

In later years on the Tour, I would often play practice rounds with friends like Tom Watson and Andy North. Some of my fondest memories of those practice rounds revolve around creating exaggerated shots over, under, and around obstacles. We had a game that was much like playing HORSE in basketball. The leader would pick a challenging shot—such as starting a tee shot at an object, like a hotel or water tower located way to the right of the fairway—and hit a big hook, and land the ball on the fairway. Besides being a lot of fun, these games really taught us how to better work the ball and learn how much we could bend a shot if we needed to during a round.

It is also important to learn to hit high shots and low shots. High shots can be valuable when teeing off downwind. Getting the ball higher in the air will let the wind be your friend and provide added distance off the tee. Additionally, you can use a high shot if the pin is tucked closely behind a bunker or in a corner of the green and you need to stop the ball quickly.

Low shots come in handy when you're hitting into the wind or in situations where the pin is located at the back of a green. In this case, you can land the ball short of the pin and let it roll out to the hole without risk of hitting the ball over the green.

Hitting high shots and low shots is a matter of ball position. Put the ball farther forward in your stance to hit a high shot. This position effectively opens the clubface at impact, causing the ball to fly higher.

For low shots, place the ball farther back in your stance. This position de-lofts the club at impact, and the ball flies lower. Low shots are actually more of a punch than a full swing.

The story of Ben Hogan is a good illustration of how critical it is to learn to work the golf ball. Early in his career, Hogan struggled because he could only hit the ball from right to left. He often mentioned how he couldn't even play certain dogleg holes because of his severe hook. He was competitive, but only after he learned to confidently work the ball from left to right was he able to become one of the great shotmakers and players of all time.

Continuing the U of H NCAA Dynasty

The week after Trevino taught me to hit a fade, I used that newfound knowledge at the NCAA Championships in Columbus, Ohio, at Ohio State's Scarlett Golf Course. Once again, we were defending champions and favored to win. As captain of the team, there was more pressure on me to perform individually. Additionally, this would be my last tournament playing for the Cougars.

My new arsenal of high fades helped me to make up a five-shot deficit in the final round and eke out a one-stroke victory over Lanny

Proud member of the U of H Golf Team

Wadkins for the individual championship. To this day, Lanny swears that I chipped in on him many times during that round. The truth is I did chip in twice. Both shots were over bunkers with very little green between the edge and the hole. There may have been a little bit of luck involved, but sometimes it's better to be lucky than good. As a team, we once again beat Wake Forest for our second consecutive championship and our twelfth in the last 15 years. There could not have been a better way to close my college golf career.

The U of H Golf Team would go on to win another four NCAA titles over the years. The Coogs are second on the list of college teams with the most NCAA golf championships, after Yale, who won their last title in 1943. Yale won 21 championships, starting with their first in 1897. The list of PGA Tour professionals who went through the program at Houston is impressive: Phil Rogers, Jacky Cupit, Kermit Zarley, Marty Fleckman, Homero Blancas, Fuzzy Zoeller, Bruce Lietzke, Ed Fiori, Fred Couples, Bill Rogers, Steve Elkington, Keith Fergus, Blaine McCallister, Tom Jenkins, and my current Golf Channel teammate, Billy Ray Brown. Even Sir Nick Faldo spent a brief time as a Cougar golfer. It is an honor for me to be a part of this legacy.

> The Houston Cougars are second on the list of college teams with the most NCAA golf championships.

With that kind of record, it is only fitting that the Golf Coaches Association of America has named its Coach of the Year Award after Dave Williams. He was still coaching when Houston won its last NCAA in 1985, and retired two years later in 1987. Coach Williams passed away in 1988 at the age of 80. He left an incredible legacy at the University of Houston and had a major role in the evolution of college golf.

Back on campus, I completed my degree requirements and graduated with a BA in Psychology. It was quite a challenge to graduate on time while playing golf at the highest collegiate level, but this was my goal when I first walked on campus. Even with my golf record, my getting a degree was the most important thing to my parents, since both of them were forced to drop out of college because of World War II. My father went into the service and my mother helped with USO events. Like so many others of that Greatest Generation, their greatest desire was for their child to get the college degree that had been denied them. They were pleased about my golf achievements but were ecstatic that I graduated and did so in four years. So it was extremely satisfying to leave Houston with both my degree and a successful golf record.

*Never bet with anyone
you meet on the first tee who
has a deep suntan, a 1-iron in
his bag, and squinty eyes.*

—DAVE MARR, JR.

CHAPTER 3

Transitioning from Amateur to Pro

Returning home to Kerrville after graduating in the spring of 1970, my plans were to again play in the various summer amateur tournaments on the East Coast and take a shot at qualifying for the US Walker Cup team. The Walker Cup is a biennial event that matches the best amateur golfers in the US against their counterparts in Great Britain and Ireland. The 1971 event was being played at the Old Course at St. Andrews. Being one of the top amateurs in the country, I was looking forward to having a chance both to compete for the United States and to play at St. Andrews.

My plan was to use these events to prepare for a try at the PGA Tour School in the fall of 1971. This is how I outlined my summer to my father one evening when he asked me what I planned to do now that I was out of college. His response was that these plans were all well and good, but he wondered how I intended to pay for them. He was very honest and straightforward.

My parents had always supported everything I did. They paid for all of my junior golf and for everything that my college scholarship didn't cover. They provided a car while I was in college and often helped subsidize the Houston golf team by covering gas expenses when we traveled to various tournaments. My dad explained that he and my mother had sacrificed greatly to help me achieve my dreams to this point, but now it was time for me to decide what I wanted to do and make my own way. It was time for me to grow up and begin to take responsibility for my life in the real world.

As usual, my dad was absolutely correct. It was time to cut the apron strings and find a way to earn a living, hopefully by playing golf. The good news was that during the 1970s, prize money continued to grow on the Tour. Average purses grew from a little under $125,000 at the end of the sixties to around $250,000.

Through the recommendation of an uncle of a high school friend, a door opened, and I was able to land a position as an assistant golf professional at Champions Golf Club back in Houston. Note the word *professional*. I was no longer an amateur golfer.

Turning pro deprived me of the chance to play on the Walker Cup or in the US Amateur that year, but my dad was right. I needed to move on. The job at Champions would be a stepping-stone and would allow me to prepare for the PGA Tour Qualifying School later that year.

The Uniqueness of Champions Golf Club

Champions Golf Club was founded in 1957 by Jimmy Demaret and Jackie Burke. The name *Champions* was derived from the fact that they were both Masters champions. Demaret won three green jackets, in 1940, 1947, and 1950. Jackie Burke won the Masters in 1956, the same year he also won the PGA Championship.

Jackie Burke winning the 1961 Flint Open

Champions is a true golfer's club. There are no tennis courts, and a prospective member must have a minimum of a 14 handicap. Members play the ball down and putt everything out. Over the years, Champions has played host to the US Open, the Ryder Cup, the Tour Championship, and a host of high-level amateur tournaments, including the annual Champions Cup.

At that time, Champions provided a venue for a select group of University of Houston golfers to work on their game in preparation for a career on the PGA Tour. Additionally, it provided exposure to the business of running a golf operation in the event that tournament golf didn't work out. To be perfectly honest, I had no interest in running a golf operation. My goal was to compete on the PGA Tour.

James Newton Demaret was a golfing original. Without a doubt, both literally and figuratively, he was one of the most colorful personalities to ever play the game. Born in Houston in 1910, Demaret grew up working as a caddie at River Oaks Country Club, where he worked for Jack Burke Sr. In addition to his caddying duties, Demaret was enlisted to be a babysitter for Burke's young son, Jackie, a role that Demaret claims he never relinquished even later on in life. Thus began a lifelong friendship between Demeret and the younger Burke.

Demaret honed his game in Galveston, where he learned to play in the windy conditions that were prevalent on that barrier island. He won his first professional tournament in 1938, and over the next 20 years, he would be a dominant fixture in professional golf. Like many athletes during that era, he took time off during the peak of his career to serve in the Navy during World War II.

The next time you see someone at your local golf course wearing lime-green slacks topped off with a lavender shirt and a plum-colored sweater, you can thank Jimmy Demaret. When Demaret broke into pro golf, the golf course landscape was the only thing with any color. Players typically wore muted outfits of grays and beiges, but being the

Ben Hogan and Jimmy Demaret
1940 Masters

son of a house painter who mixed his own paint colors, Demaret was having none of that. He famously visited a women's clothing designer in New York and ordered a golf wardrobe that was a rainbow of colors and a variety of styles. He abandoned the traditional fedora and wore an assortment of hat styles, including one that looked like it belonged on a railroad engineer from Oz.

Demaret was also the first, and almost the last, player to wear short pants in a professional tournament. On the day he wore them, the combination of the cut and the material used in his custom-made shorts left little to the imagination, especially when Jimmy crouched down to line up a putt. The PGA quickly issued an edict that slacks were the preferred form of dress. Forrest Fezler did try to challenge this rule years later by changing into shorts in a port-a-potty on the 18th hole at the 1983 US Open at Oakmont. To my knowledge, that was the last time any player wore shorts in a professional golf tournament.

Demaret had a professional-quality singing voice and was an exceptional stand-up comic. He would routinely entertain golf fans during the day and nightclub customers by night. He was a popular figure who was known to even make Ben Hogan chuckle. He had a bevy of friends from the entertainment industry, like Bing Crosby, Bob Hope, Phil Harris, and Lucille Ball. He also cohosted the very popular television show *Shell's Wonderful World of Golf* with fellow legend Gene Sarazen. Demaret was always the showman, with an infectious smile and engaging personality.

On top of all of those qualities, Demaret could play. Besides his three Masters victories, he won 28 other PGA Tour events. He won six times in both 1940 and 1947. In the 1940 Masters, he shot 30 on the back nine on Sunday to win by 4 shots. He played on three Ryder Cup teams and never lost a match. He was inducted into the World Golf Hall of Fame in 1983.

Describing Onion Creek Golf Club, Demaret said that God put it there; all he did was manicure it.

Besides co-founding Champions Golf Club, perhaps Demaret's most lasting legacy to the game was an event he started in 1978. Four years earlier, in 1974, Jimmy teamed with another friend, Jimmy Connolly, and built a course that he painted into the central Texas countryside on the southeast side of Austin. Describing Onion Creek Golf Club, Demaret said that God put it there; all Jimmy did was manicure it. In 1978, he hosted a tournament at Onion Creek for players over 50 years of age, on the assumption that spectators would be interested in seeing these

Legends of Golf back in action. Boy, were they ever. Not only did this tournament grow in popularity, but it was the genesis of what we now call the Champions Tour.

Demeret's partner in founding Champions was Jackie Burke Jr. Thirteen years younger than Demaret, Burke grew up in a golfing family. His dad, who was born in Philadelphia, finished second in the 1920 US Open. Jack Burke Sr. was a well-respected player during his era. However, he learned that he could make a better living teaching the game, rather than competing for the meager prize money that was available back then. He became the head pro at Houston's River Oaks Country Club in the mid-1920s and quickly established himself as one of the most sought-after teaching pros in the country.

Jackie Burke Jr. grew up around the golf course and the caddie yard, where he developed his skills under the watchful eye of his father. He turned pro at age 19 and notched 9 of his 16 tournament wins

> Champions Golf Club was founded in 1957 by Jimmy Demaret and Jackie Burke.

between 1950 and 1952, including 4 in a row. His best year on Tour was 1956, when he won both the Masters and the PGA Championship. Burke also has an extensive Ryder Cup résumé. He played on five teams, was playing captain in 1957, and served as an assistant captain to Hal Sutton in 2004. Jackie was inducted into the Golf Hall of Fame in 2000 and received the PGA Tour Lifetime Achievement award in 2004.

Burke and Demaret were total opposites. Burke was as reticent at Demaret was flamboyant. Burke typified work, while Demaret personified fun.

True Characters

In the evenings Demaret would often hold court at the bar in the spacious locker room at Champions, recalling outrageous tales of his contemporaries on the Tour. He spoke of players and entertainers like Walter Hagen, Ky Laffoon, "Lighthorse Harry" Cooper, Lefty Stackhouse, Phil Harris, Bing Crosby, and many, many more. I remember a few of the stories, like the time when Ky Laffoon dragged an uncooperative sand wedge behind his car on his drive from Houston to San Antonio to teach it a lesson.

Demaret told of the psychological games that Walter Hagen would play to put his opponents off guard. For example, "The Haig" was known to crawl out of a Rolls-Royce that had pulled up to the first tee just minutes before his starting time. Wearing a tuxedo and acting hungover, Hagen would give the impression that he had been out all night, luring his opponent into a false sense of security. Of course, this would disappear when Hagen striped his tee shot down the middle of the fairway.

Demaret also recounted the tale of the tempestuous Lefty Stackhouse, who had a fistfight with a rosebush after hitting a duck hook off a tee, which cost him a tournament. Lefty's intent was to punish his right hand for causing the hook. When that hand was sufficiently bloody, he looked at his left hand and said, "Don't think you're getting off easy," and proceeded to bash that hand against the rosebush as well.

Ky Laffoon dragged an uncooperative sand wedge behind his car on his drive from Houston to San Antonio to teach it a lesson.

I wish I had had the foresight to have written down more of those stories, as they could easily fill another book. It was beneficial for me to meet the bevy of celebrities who passed through Champions so early in my pro career, as many of them either hosted or participated in PGA Tour events. It would create some great opportunities in the future.

As I saw it, in contrast to Demaret, Jack Burke was harsher and a real taskmaster. At that time on the Tour, Lee Trevino and Frank Beard seemed to be winning tournaments in alternating weeks. Lee was a fader of the ball (preferring a left-to-right shot), while Frank preferred the draw (a right-to-left ball flight). Burke instructed us assistant pros to gear the lessons we gave the members to coincide with whichever player won on a particular week. If Trevino won, we would teach a fade. If Beard won, we would teach a draw. It must have been very confusing for the members.

Don't get me wrong—Jackie was, and is, a well-respected teacher. Through the years, he has helped many established Tour players, such as Ben Crenshaw, Hal Sutton, Steve Elkington, and Phil Mickelson. He has his own style of teaching, especially putting, that many times involves physical contact. Burke stressed the importance of being anchored securely to the ground and getting down close to your business while putting. When students tried to emulate this stance, they would sometimes find themselves flat on their back, a result of a Burke forearm shiver. Standing with their head down, trying to get closer to the green, they would never see him coming as he demonstrated the obvious weakness in their stance.

Jack's brother, Jimmy Burke, was the general manager at Champions and served as something of a buffer at the club. When Jack would stir the pot, Jimmy Burke had the knack of being able to smooth things over pretty much to everyone's satisfaction. He showed me how to handle my duties in the pro shop. We were all deeply saddened when Jimmy was killed in an automobile accident in 1990. We lost a true friend and colleague. I miss his quick smile and dry wit. Champions was never the same without his wisecracking in the pro shop.

Champions was a great place for a young professional. Celebrities, Tour players, and all sorts of successful business types passed through to play and visit. Every day, there was the chance to meet someone you saw in the movies, saw on TV, or read about in the newspapers. It was the perfect place to play, practice, learn, and make the transition from amateur to golf professional.

Meanwhile on the national scene, the advent of the 1970s saw another slight shift in golf's hierarchy. The decade was totally dominated by Jack Nicklaus. The Golden Bear won eight major championships during that time span, and Gary Player and Lee Trevino won four majors each. Speaking of Trevino, "The Merry Mex," as he was known, won 21 times in the '70s—including those four majors—gaining popularity on the level of the Big Three of Palmer, Nicklaus, and Player.

*Competitive golf
is played mainly on a
five-and-a-half-inch course ...
the space between your ears.*
—BOBBY JONES

CHAPTER 4

BEN HOGAN

My time at Champions was spent working in the golf shop, practicing, and playing various mini tour events in places like Mexico, Atlanta, and Florida. The next PGA Tour Qualifying School was in the fall of 1971, and I was using these tournaments to keep a competitive edge while selling golf balls and posting tee times.

The Houston Champions International was a PGA Tour event that was held at Champions from 1966 to 1971. This event is now called the Shell Houston Open. As tournament week approached in 1971, preparations were in full swing. One day the pro shop was buzzing because we heard Ben Hogan was coming in for some early practice rounds.

This was exciting. Hogan was nearing the end of his playing career, and rarely played at all. However, he had finished ninth at this tournament the previous year. I was hoping to meet him since I'd actually learned to play golf by practicing the fundamentals he outlined in his book. I also hoped to get his autograph on my well-worn copy.

One evening after work I received a telephone call from Richard Killian, another assistant pro, asking if I would like to join Jimmy Demaret, Jack Burke, and Ben Hogan for a round of golf the following morning.

Perfection by Ben Hogan

Was this a trick question? I was a bit suspicious, as Richard loved to play practical jokes. I wasn't sure if I should believe him or not, but I thought it best to play it safe and show up in the morning for the tee time.

A Life-Changing Encounter

The next day, on the first tee of the Cypress Creek Course at Champions, I said good morning to my two employers and turned to look into the ice-blue eyes of my idol, Ben Hogan. My life changed forever that day.

Hogan was slightly taller than my 5 foot 8. For a small man, he had large wrists and hands, with powerful-looking forearms. He was dressed in a light blue golf shirt and gray pleated slacks. His custom-made black golf shoes were highly polished. He was wearing the white cap that had become his trademark. He was tan and lean and had the look of a very confident man. He greeted me with a steely, piercing stare, extended his hand, and said, "Good morning, son. I'm Ben Hogan." His handshake was firm, and I noticed his hand was hard and calloused and rough, like someone who had done lots of manual labor.

> "Good morning, son. I'm Ben Hogan."
> —Ben Hogan

Introductions done, the three of them decided on a game that, given my financial situation at the time, would likely put me in debt forever if I lost. As the round progressed, however, I was totally unaware of the match, as I couldn't take my eyes off Ben Hogan.

I was in awe of the swing I'd worked so hard to mimic. Hogan was a machine. He was 61 years old at the time and hit the ball as solidly as anyone I'd ever seen. The sound of the club striking the ball was different from any sound I'd ever heard on a golf course. His ball flight was remarkable. To this day, I can still see the ball tracking like a laser beam against the gray Texas sky.

As we played on, I became more relaxed and made birdies at the par-3 eighth and par-5 ninth. Unfortunately, the skies opened up as we walked off the ninth green, and heavy thunderstorms chased us off the golf course for the rest of the day. So we went inside to calculate the scores and settle up on the team match. I shot 32 on the front nine—Mr. Hogan shot 33.

Hogan huddled with Burke and Demaret in the corner of the locker room, and occasionally, one of them would raise his head and stare at me. I felt as though I'd committed some heinous crime and was watching the jury deliberate my fate. Finally, Hogan walked over to me and said he would like to continue the game tomorrow if I could be available. I looked over to Burke and Demaret, and they both nodded yes. What a thrill to play two days in a row with one's hero! Yes, I would be back tomorrow.

After a steady all-night rain, the morning brought overcast skies and strong gusty winds out of the south. Play on the golf course that day would be most difficult, with the finishing holes directly into the wind. Again, I paid little attention to the team aspect of our match and concentrated on the individual game. The day dictated lots of pars sprinkled with a few birdies but very few bogeys or higher. Despite the conditions, Mr. Hogan carded a 2-under-par 70 to my 71.

> "I didn't ask if you were a member of the Tour; I asked if you would like to play Colonial next week!"
> —Ben Hogan

As we made our way to the locker room to tally up the results, I felt a bit out of place as the three of them huddled again by one of the lockers. After what seemed an eternity, Mr. Hogan walked over and said if I came to the club for dinner, we would settle up for the match. This was not an invitation to dine with him, but a summons to be in the restaurant at 7:00 p.m. I had no idea what to expect that evening and certainly did not know that it would change my life so dramatically.

I was sitting in the dining room that evening, finishing my dessert, when Mr. Hogan walked in and approached my table. He came right to the point. "Son, would you like to play in the Colonial Invitational next week in Fort Worth?" My reply, "Mr. Hogan, I'm not a member of the Tour," was met with his retort, "I didn't ask if you were a member of the Tour; I asked if you would like to play Colonial next week!" Sheepishly I answered, "Yes, sir, I would."

He disappeared into Jimmy Demaret's office for about 15 minutes and then returned to where I was seated. He must have been a wonderful gambler because I could read nothing in his actions or expression. Then his face broke into a big smile, and he said, "You're in."

I couldn't believe it. Not only had I just had two glorious days playing golf with Ben Hogan, but now I was also getting the chance to play in a PGA Tour event at "Hogan's Alley," Colonial Country Club. But his voice interrupted my exhilaration when he said, "There is one stipulation, however—you must play your practice rounds only with me." I couldn't believe what I was hearing. It didn't seem real, but it was.

From that day forward, my golfing career was unmistakably linked to Ben Hogan. The man who unknowingly taught me how to play golf through his book would become my mentor, sponsor, and great friend.

"There is one stipulation. You must play your practice rounds only with me."
—Ben Hogan

Sadly, that tournament in Houston was the last time Ben Hogan would play competitive golf. In the first round, he twisted his knee on the par-3 third hole while trying to play his ball from a hazard. He limped around the front nine in 44. As he was trying to hit his tee shot on 11, that knee gave out, causing him to slip. Following that shot, he instructed his caddie to pick up his ball, shook hands with his playing partners, and rode back to the clubhouse in a golf cart. It was a sad and abrupt end to one of the greatest careers in the history of the game.

Golf Course Management

Despite the circumstances in Houston, Ben Hogan was a man of his word, and just the two of us played all my practice rounds the following week at Colonial. Having won the tournament five times, his objective was to teach me his own plan of attack. Colonial is a golf course that requires precision, preparation, and patience. He emphasized this to me in each practice round and made suggestions on how to play certain key holes. Watching him play was magical, with his balance and control over every shot.

I was learning by observing, and occasionally he would make a subtle suggestion. On the third hole, for instance, I pulled out a 2-iron for my second shot into the green. He suggested that a 4-wood might be a better shot. I thought the 2-iron was plenty, and hit the shot. The ball landed on the front of the green and raced to the back edge. He threw another ball down and said, "Now hit your 4-wood and fade it in. You see, this green seems to always be firm and won't hold a shot with a lower trajectory."

I hit the 4-wood with the fade, and the ball sat down in the middle of the green. Lesson learned!

During the practice rounds at Colonial, he taught me such things as never to go for the par-5 first hole in two. Since tall trees surround the green on that hole, it doesn't get proper sun, leaving the surrounding area scraggly. If you try to reach that green in two and miss, you may end up with a difficult lie and have trouble getting up and down. The better strategy is to lay up and play a full wedge for the third shot. As stated before, Hogan pointed out that the green at the third hole is always firmer than most, so the second shot would require a high fade to keep the ball on the putting surface. He also taught me never to fly the tee shot onto the green at the par-3 fourth. The green on that hole is also hard, and it's difficult to stop the ball. If your ball goes over the green, you're dead. The better play is to hit short of the pin and allow the ball to work back to the hole. If the ball lands too short, it's a fairly easy up and down to save par.

Years later I was playing a practice round at Colonial with Ben Crenshaw. The course was backed up when we reached that fourth hole. As we waited to play, I related to Gentle Ben how Hogan thought the hole should be played, and asked his opinion. Crenshaw said all he did was take out a 1-iron and hit it as high as he could. Interesting. Considering that I couldn't hit a 1-iron more than head high, I told him that I would stick with Hogan's approach. He found this to be quite humorous, and to this day, when we revisit some events of the past, just the mention of Colonial brings this story to the surface. Ben always laughs and merely says, "Just take out a 1-iron and hit it as high as you can! It's just that simple." Maybe that's true for a handful of players like Ben Crenshaw, but for most mortals, that shot simply does not exist.

> "Now hit your 4-wood and fade it in."
> —Ben Hogan

It's All in the Details

From my first experience with Mr. Hogan at the 1971 Colonial, I learned the value of the practice round and the importance of using that opportunity to discover the nuances of a golf course—like learning the best place to hit the ball, what areas to avoid, how putts break, and the best place to land shots on the green. The practice round is vital to success in a tournament. Without a serious practice round, you may as well play the first round of a tournament in the dark.

Hogan was legendary for his meticulous preparation for a tournament. For example, since he had learned to become more of a left-to-right player, each year he would spend the week before the Masters at Seminole Golf Club in Florida. During this week he would practice hitting all the shots he would encounter, but especially the right-to-left shots he would need to score at Augusta.

I embraced this philosophy and used it throughout my career. I always thought previewing a golf course the way I learned from Ben Hogan gave me an advantage over my competitors. I always thought I was one of the best-prepared players on the Tour. That is, until I met Bernhard Langer.

Langer and I teamed together in one of the early Shark Shootouts played on the outskirts of Los Angeles. It would take us forever to play our practice rounds, as Bernhard was always stepping off distances, measuring, or figuring something out on the course or around the green. He probably had a yardage from the door handle on every port-a-potty. At the time I thought it was overkill. How wrong I was! Once the tournament started, I can't tell you how many times he helped me with carry yardages, breaks on the greens, and even club selection. As partners we could confer on all of those things, and he was quite an asset. I think we finished in a tie for second that year. It's easy to see why he was so valuable in Ryder Cup play for Europe.

> I always thought I was one of the best-prepared players on the Tour. That is, until I met Bernhard Langer.

Bernhard Langer is a great competitor, golf partner, and friend. He certainly taught me to pay more attention to detail. It's no surprise to me that he's continued to be a major force on the Champions Tour. From my vantage point in the Golf Channel tower, I've had the honor of watching this true tactician decimate some very difficult golf courses with his precise and course management. Langer's mastery of the game is impressive to see.

The bottom line is you can't overprepare to play golf. Success on the golf course is the result of what you invest off the course, in the gym, on the range, and in practice rounds.

After finishing my practice rounds at Colonial with Ben Hogan, my thoughts drifted back to the week before at Champions. Mr. Hogan allowed me to watch him practice after I'd played that round and a half with him. His friends, Jimmy Demaret and Jackie Burke, let him practice on a fairway on the Jack Rabbit Course—the second 18 at Champions—to allow him to have more privacy. With a full bag of practice balls and caddie in tow, he'd hit balls for hours. I was impressed with not only his repetitive swing but also the unbelievable variety of shots he could hit. He would hit high shots and low shots. He would first draw the ball and then fade it. Then he would practice hitting shots a particular distance with multiple clubs. His caddie rarely had to move to retrieve the ball. The sound of contact at impact was incredible. Every shot sounded solid. Every one! The obvious point was to learn to be versatile and have more than one way to play a shot.

> Success on the golf course is the result of what you invest off the course.

When the Colonial finally started, Mr. Hogan disappeared. I didn't see him anywhere. I played well and made the cut with ease, but still no Hogan. He was also conspicuously absent that weekend. I used the strategy learned from our practice rounds, played well, and just missed finishing in the top ten.

During the tournament, I was approached by a reporter from the local newspaper in Fort Worth. The reporter asked what I thought about Hubert Green winning the tournament in Houston the previous week. Hubert was a rookie on the Tour that year and would actually go on to win Rookie of the Year for 1971. I told him that Hubert's victory showed how strong the Tour was getting, since anyone had the ability to win in any given week.

The next day the headline in his story read, "Mahaffey Says If Hubert Green Can Win A Golf Tournament, Anybody Can." When Hubert saw me in the locker room at Colonial that day, he took me aside and gave me a chance to explain what I'd actually said. He then told me to always be careful of what I say to the press and to never give them a chance to misinterpret anything. That lesson stayed with me throughout my career.

Later on, Hubert Green became one of my very best friends. Over the years, along with Fuzzy Zoeller, we played more practice rounds than I can count.

Hogan finally called on Sunday night. He started by telling me that I did all right but got ahead of myself several times during the week. Then he went into specific instances and detail. How did he know? He wasn't even there. Or was he? He concluded our conversation by saying he would like to see me in his office at the Ben Hogan Company in Fort Worth at 10:30 Monday morning.

A Dream Come True

Arriving early, I was greeted by a delightful lady who was Mr. Hogan's secretary. At precisely 10:30, she escorted me into the office—where Hogan was seated behind his desk, wearing a coat and tie and smoking a cigarette. He directed me to sit down. Then he stared at me for an unbelievably long time, smoking and seemingly in deep thought. Finally he said, "John, I want to sign you to a contract to represent my company. I'll provide you with all you'll need to play. Everything will be under my personal supervision. My own clubmaker, Gene Sheeley, will be making your clubs."

> "John, I want to sign you to a contract to represent my company."
> —Ben Hogan

I was totally dumbfounded. So much was happening so fast. In the space of two weeks, I had gone from a world of selling golf balls in the Champions Pro Shop to playing in the Colonial to being offered the opportunity to represent equipment manufactured by my idol.

He reached inside his desk drawer and pulled out two copies of a one-page contract. He slid them over to me to read. The contract outlined what he had told me, stated in simple terms. He said that if I agreed, I should sign them both, one copy for him and one for me. I asked if I could make a phone call to Houston with the news. He said of course and that it would be in my best interest to have my lawyer check out the contract as well. The call to Houston went well, and I read the brief contract to my lawyer. The lawyer said OK but even though it appeared that everything was in order, he would like to review it in his office. I was very excited and went back to tell Mr. Hogan. We agreed that I should sign the contracts in Houston after my lawyer read them in person and that I should mail Mr. Hogan his copy.

Unbelievable! How great it was going to be to represent the Ben Hogan Company and to have a master clubmaker overseeing the grinding and assembling of my clubs. Quality control was most important to the Hogan Company, and everyone there took it very seriously. Even though clubs were mass-produced, the raw iron and wood heads were not always as precisely formed as they are today. As a result you needed a true artist to shape them to your specifications. What a bonus!

> How ironic that I was going to have custom-made Hogan clubs.

When I was 14 years old, I had outgrown the set of clubs I'd borrowed from my uncle. I bought my first set of clubs with money I'd earned caddying. I played with that used set of PowerBilts until I wore them out. I tried out all kinds of clubs to replace them and finally settled on a set of Hogan clubs that seemed to fit me better and felt more solid. I used those clubs all through high school and well into my university years. How ironic that now I was going to have custom-made Hogan clubs.

Early on I'd developed an avid interest in golf clubs and what made them tick. I learned how to make minor repairs, change grips, and set the lies and lofts throughout a set of irons to fit my specifications. Over time I became very anal about my clubs, almost to the point of obsession. At the Ben Hogan factory I would eventually learn everything about building a set of clubs from beginning to end. This was dangerous information. As a result, for most of my career, no one but myself or Gene Sheeley would make any repairs to my equipment. At the height of my career, I built an incredible workshop in my home, with tools that would rival those of many golf club manufacturers.

The Need for Experience

The celebration in his office was cut short as Mr. Hogan definitely had an agenda. "Now there are a few things we need to discuss concerning your level of experience and approach to the game in competition," he said. He continued with an almost hole-by-hole critique of my play at Colonial. It was constructive criticism, but I kept wondering how he knew when he hadn't even been there? I found out much later that he'd had friends charting every shot I'd hit. His wife, Valerie, had been there as well. He had also come out, in disguise, on Sunday to watch the finishing holes.

Even though I had a Tour quality golf course at Champions where I could play and practice, what I really needed was more tournament experience and competition. The mistakes I'd made in Fort Worth could be all but eliminated by playing more events. With PGA Tour qualifying coming at the end of the year, I had to get busy finding places to play. So with contracts in hand, I left for Houston.

> I realized how right Hogan had been about needing more experience.

Back home, after some research I was fortunate to find a couple of opportunities to play. One was called the Peter Jackson Canadian Tour. It had been started by the tobacco company of the same name, and it consisted of seven to eight events played across Canada. The other was the Florida Mini Tour: a series of tournaments in South Florida. I hoped that playing on both of these tours would help make me more tournament tough.

The first of the Canadian events was played in Winnipeg. To get there I drove due north from Houston for what seemed like an eternity. The rest of the Canadian tournaments were scattered across the continent in places named Kamloops, Moose Jaw, Regina, and Calgary. The final two tournaments were played in Vancouver.

Canada was a lot of fun, and I felt that I gained valuable experience there. Traveling across the country gave me a taste of what Tour travel and preparation was going to be like. I met some great people and stayed with some very hospitable families, such as Bud and Pidge Loftus in Vancouver. Bud was a golf professional in Canada and his whole family was in the golf business. We all spent many evenings talking about golf, equipment, and my relationship with Ben Hogan. The Loftus family was super to me.

My game got better up north. No wins yet, but I'd started to make money. More importantly, I was gaining confidence as each part of the world offered new lessons.

After Canada I went to Florida to play in a few events, continue building confidence, and gain more experience. A lady by the name of Millie Mix had organized a series of tournaments that became known as the Florida Mini Tour. It would be another opportunity to learn more about life on the road. I found that life in the real world was certainly different from the more sheltered life that had been amateur golf. Tour golf meant constantly adjusting to different conditions, from grasses and sand densities to climates and time zones. I thought the Florida Tour would be easy pickings, but it wasn't. I found there were a lot of players I'd never heard of who could really score. Not only did I not win one of the handful of events that I played, but I barely made expenses. It was another tough lesson in what was going to be a long learning process. I realized how right Hogan had been about needing more experience. I had to regroup, refocus, and quickly elevate my game. Time was running out as Tour School was fast approaching.

The Best in the Business

After playing in these two mini tours, I felt I needed to visit Mr. Hogan in Fort Worth to give him an update and pick up the new clubs Gene Sheeley had made to my specifications. Mr. Hogan met me in

> Having Hogan personally inspect a set of golf clubs is an exercise in quality control that can't be duplicated by a machine or computer.

his office late one morning. He summoned Gene to the office, instructing him to bring my new clubs. While waiting he asked what else I'd planned until Tour qualifying. I told him that I'd entered one more tournament before Tour school and was anxious to try the new clubs.

Gene came into the office and handed the clubs directly to Mr. Hogan, who took them one by one, checking them from every angle you could imagine. He asked about the swing weights, the shafts, the lies, and the lofts. Gene handed him a sheet of paper with all the information included. Mr. Hogan perused the paper, nodded, and then asked Gene if he had made three sets as directed. Gene said he had, so Hogan said, "OK then, Gene, bring me the other two sets. I'm not happy with the look of the 8-iron in this set. The woods are fine." Mr. Hogan then shared with me that the 8-iron was the most difficult club to fit to the look he preferred in the rest of the irons. This particular 8-iron was a bit too rounded toward the toe of the club and didn't blend in with the head shapes of the rest of the set.

After Gene returned from the factory with the other two sets, Mr. Hogan examined them as meticulously as he had the first. He selected the two sets he liked best and handed them to me with instructions to practice with both. Then I was to pick the one I hit best to take with me on the road and keep the other as a backup. With new clubs under my arm, I thanked them both for everything and drove to Houston.

Engineering and quality control have evolved significantly since those days. Today's clubmaking rivals airplane design. At the end of the day, however, one thing stayed the same: the most important consideration in golf club design is how the club looks and feels in the hands of the person using it.

Hogan's attention to detail in the products he produced was almost as legendary as his golf swing. He believed that if he put his name on a product, that product was a representation of his values. He never accepted anything but the best, and his equipment reflected that standard. When he first began his clubmaking business, he threw out the entire first batch of clubs produced in his factory as they did not meet his standard.

> I was very nervous but somehow scored well enough to win. It was my first tournament win as a professional.

The old Hogan factory on West Pafford in Fort Worth may seem archaic when compared to today's clubmaking facilities, but one thing that can't be replaced is Ben Hogan's eye. Having him personally inspect a set of golf clubs is an exercise in quality control that can't be duplicated by a machine or computer.

After two weeks of practicing back in Houston, I left for Sandy Springs, Georgia, which is just outside of Atlanta, to play in a tournament consisting of a small cross-section of golf pros from across the country. This would be my last competition before Tour qualifying. I played well all week, and on the first day, I ended up in the final pairing with Tommy Aaron, who would go on to win the Masters in 1973. I was very nervous that day but somehow scored well enough to win. It was my first tournament win as a professional.

The new Hogan clubs felt great. It was the first set of golf clubs that were made especially for me. When I set up to the ball the irons looked perfect. I felt confident with my equipment and confident with my game. I was ready for Tour Qualifying School.

When I got back to Houston, I needed to send my application for qualifying school to the PGA Tour office. The application required letters of recommendation from three current members in good standing who felt I had the game to compete on the Tour. It was such an honor to have Ben Hogan, Jimmy Demaret, and Jack Burke provide them.

At that time, there were several stages to go through to qualify for a PGA Tour card. Fortunately, I had little problem making it through the regional events. Then came the most gut-wrenching time I was ever to experience in golf. The final test was held that year at the PGA National Golf Club in Palm Beach Gardens, Florida. If you didn't make it through the final qualifying tournament, you had to wait a whole year to try again. There were eight rounds to be played, and the number of Tour cards given out would be determined by the quality of the field. Not knowing the exact number of spots just added to the pressure. I'd never experienced such anxiety.

> BEN HOGAN
>
> July 8, 1971
>
> Tournament Players Division
> Professional Golfers' Assn. of America
> Lincoln Building
> 60 East 42nd Street
> New York, New York 10017
>
> Gentlemen:
>
> This letter is my personal recommendation for John Mahaffey's admittance to the PGA school and participation in the qualifying trials.
>
> I have played several rounds of golf with him and I found him to be a gentleman of the highest character and an excellent player.
>
> Sincerely
>
> Ben Hogan
>
> VIA AIRMAIL

I had a shaky start, but I'd settled down by the halfway point and was in good position entering the last four rounds. During the fifth round on the ninth hole, I hit my tee shot into a fairway bunker but had a good lie. Nine was a long par-4, playing into the wind, with the second shot over water. I hit a 4-wood out of the trap onto the green, made my par, and didn't think much about it at the time.

Champions Golf Club

July 1, 1971

TO WHOM IT MAY CONCERN:

It has been my pleasure to watch the progress of John Mahaffey, both as a player and person. This note is my personal recommendation for this young man to enter your school and qualification trials – he is an excellent player.

JACK BURKE
President

Champions Golf Club

July 12, 1971

Tournament Players Division
National P.G.A.
Palm Beach Garden, Florida

n. Texas 77040 · A.C. 713. 444 · 6262

Dear Sir:

I have known John Mahaffey for five or six years, and he has been associated with Jack Burke and myself here at Champions the past couple of years.

John is well qualified in every capacity of golf, and I see a very bright future for him and I am sure he will be a credit to his profession.

Sincerely,

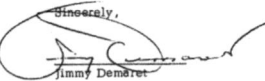

Jimmy Demaret

JD/mb

P.O. Box 40280 · Houston. Texas 77040 · A.C. 713. 444 · 6262

Spies in the Gallery

That evening I got a phone call from Gardner Dickinson, who was a Tour winner and close friend of Ben Hogan. Gardner lived in the area and had been recruited by Hogan to watch me and report back to him nightly as I progressed through the tournament. Gardner said that both he and Hogan were pleased with how I'd been playing but questioned some of my on-course decisions. He referenced that shot on the ninth hole. Mr. Hogan told him to emphasize strongly to me that courting disaster could cause me to miss qualifying. If I'd not hit the 4-wood perfectly out of the bunker, I could have made a big number. The secret to qualifying was to play cautiously aggressive. It was great advice. I made a few bogeys over the next few days, but nothing higher. I walked to the final tee box needing anything less than a 10 to qualify. A routine par-4 secured my player's card. The dream that began in 1960 when Uncle Henry took me to that tournament in San Antonio was now a reality.

Among the other players who qualified with me that year were Tom Watson, Lanny Wadkins, David Graham, Leonard Thompson, and a host of others with incredible records in golf. It was arguably one of the best Tour Qualifying Schools to date—some say ever. I received a congratulatory phone call from Mr. Hogan and a directive that he would like to see me in Fort Worth when I got back to Texas.

> The dream that began in 1960 when Uncle Henry took me to that tournament in San Antonio was now a reality.

Back at the Hogan factory I was greeted by a smiling Ben Hogan. We talked for a while and then he got down to business. He began with some sage advice about the Tour. He stressed how important focus is when playing practice rounds. He suggested that I try to play practice rounds with veteran Tour players, especially those who have previously won the event. He told me to pick their brains and pay attention to the way they play each hole. Notice when they are aggressive and where they play conservatively. Study the course and formulate a strategy. Learn to not deviate from my plan. That takes discipline. Discipline takes time. And finally, he said, "Use your time wisely, be patient with yourself, and work hard but effectively. Do so and you will be successful. Keep in touch." That was it—brief but to the point. The Hogan way. I headed home.

Sage Advice

While at home in Houston in 1972, I received the schedule and credentials for my rookie year on the PGA Tour. I also had the opportunity to play a couple of rounds at Champions with Jack Burke and Jay Hebert, both former PGA Champions. I think they were curious to see if I had what it really took to play the Tour. During one of those rounds, Jay Hebert said something to me that has stuck through my whole career. He said if I played long enough on the Tour, anything that could happen would happen. It was best to always be prepared for the unpredictable.

Jay Hebert was one of the most personable gentlemen I ever met. He had been a captain in the Marines during World War II and had been wounded at Iwo Jima. Jay's brother, Lionel, also played on the Tour. They are the only brothers to have both won the PGA Championship—Jay in 1960 and Lionel in 1957. Lionel and Jay were two wonderful, fun-loving characters who grew up in Lafayette, Louisiana. They loved Cajun food and told some of the best Boudreaux and Thibodeaux jokes I've ever heard. Lionel was also quite the entertainer and would often bring out his trumpet and play with the likes of the great Boots Randolph in pro-am events.

> "Son, you had your chance to make that putt, now let us have our turn."
> —Jay Hebert

I vaguely recall one of these outings for Amana in Cedar Rapids, Iowa. While Lionel and Boots were entertaining the participants, Tom Watson and I moved to a different part of the hotel where we were singing a variety of songs, very loudly, with Bobby Goldsboro. We sang well into the night, and at no time during this performance did Bobby suggest that we give up our day jobs for a career in music. I'm not sure anyone in the hotel got much sleep that night, but I'm sure they agreed with Bobby's assessment of our singing talent. I certainly paid the price the next day on the golf course, but what a fun night.

During one of those rounds Jay also taught me a valuable lesson in golf etiquette. On one hole after missing a putt, I moved to the other side of the green and began to stroke some practice putts. Jay admonished me by saying, "Son, you had your chance to make that putt—now let us have our turn." This gentle rebuke stayed with me throughout my career, and I've always tried to be mindful of my playing partners, whether playing in the US Open or at a local pro-am.

Getting ready for my rookie year, I spent countless hours on the practice tee at Champions. During that time, I really focused on my wedge play. I learned the precise maximum distance I could hit with either my sand wedge or pitching wedge (we only carried two back then), so that any time I had a wedge in my hand, I was thinking birdie. I worked hardest on half shots so awkward distances with either wedge would no longer be problematic. Confident wedge play makes up for occasional mistakes with the long game.

My game had evolved considerably in the year since I'd graduated from Houston. I was able to work the ball around the golf course and rarely missed a fairway or a green. In years to come I would consistently be in the top ten on the Tour in fairways hit, and led the Tour in greens in regulation in both 1985 and 1986. It was about then when I realized I'd moved from being only a ball striker and had become a shotmaker. I'd learned to maneuver the ball, not just hit it solidly.

Golf is a thinking man's game.
You can have all the shots in the bag,
but if you don't know what to do with
them, you've got troubles.

—CHI CHI RODRIGUEZ

CHAPTER 5

ROOKIE YEAR

In 1972, eligibility regulations dictated that a player with my status had two ways to gain entry into a tournament: he could qualify on Monday prior to that week's tournament or receive one of the rare sponsor's exemptions. Either way, once in a tournament, the player would need to make the cut—placing in the top 70 players after two rounds—to automatically be in the field for the next event. Major championships and invitational tournaments had their own criteria for eligibility. A player finishing in the top 60 places on the end-of-the-year money list would be fully exempt from having to go through this qualifying process for the following year.

The month before the '72 season started, I was consumed with play and lots of practice. Then it came time to pack the car and leave for the first tournament, the Glen Campbell Los Angeles Open. But first came Monday qualifying at El Caballero Country Club in Tarzana, California. Since it was the first tournament after the winter layoff, there were very few spots available as most exempt players entered the tournament. Even so, there were so many players trying to qualify that the Monday qualifier had to be held at multiple courses. I played well enough to get the first alternate spot after a playoff at El Cab, but the only way I was going to get into the tournament would be if an exempt player withdrew before the first round. Fortunately for me, Lanny Wadkins did and I was in. It was a lucky break.

My first official event as a member of the PGA Tour would be played at Rancho Park, a municipal course located in downtown Los Angeles. For the record, I shot 66 in my first round and I remember thinking that it couldn't be this easy. It wasn't. I ended up finishing 30th, after my inexperience surfaced. One positive was that I'd made the cut and was exempt from having to qualify for the next week's tournament.

Golf in the Real World

The rest of the West Coast and Florida swings of the Tour were sprinkled with made and missed cuts and made and missed qualifyings. It wasn't until the middle of the season that I started becoming more consistent. After 13 straight tournaments, I arrived in Memphis, Tennessee, tired but encouraged. My game was getting better and my attitude was more positive. Hogan told me it was all part of the learning process. That week proved to be the turning point. In the final round, I shot a sweet 69 and finished alone in second place behind Lee Trevino. Most importantly, I won enough money to ensure my exemption for the next year. All in all, I had a pretty decent rookie year. I played in 32 tournaments and made the cut in 24 of them, with 4 top-ten finishes, and ended the year at number 41 on the money list.

Throughout most of the year, Mr. Hogan was brief when we talked. He would remind me that experience was always the best teacher and that you have to live through an experience to understand it. He would offer some constructive criticism but pretty much left it up to me to figure things out. I didn't get it at the time but later realized it was the best thing he could have done.

His point really hit home when I was standing over the putt on that final hole in Memphis. It was less than a foot long, but it was for outright second place. If I made the putt, I would secure my exemption for the next year. My hands were shaking and my mind was racing. Thoughts were bouncing off the inside of my skull. I backed off once to regroup and then stepped up and knocked the ball into the back of the hole. Had it not hit dead center, it would not have stayed in. You have to experience pressure to understand it.

That was Hogan's point. He wanted me to be my own man—to be able to stand on my own and not have to depend solely on someone else to mend an ailing golf game. He believed in self-help so a player could fix his own problems while on the course. I'd always respected him so much for his golf game, but now I respected him even more for his intelligence and intuition.

There were many veterans who took young players joining the Tour under their wing. In my case, these veterans included Miller Barber, Don January, and Lionel and Jay Hebert. These guys would provide advice on where to stay and where to eat, and they would help us get invited to participate in outings to help offset expenses.

Miller Barber was an absolute original. He had a unique golf swing that really worked for him. The combination of his swing, his high-pitched squeaky voice, and his secretive nature earned him the nickname Mr. X. His good nature and naïveté put him on the receiving end of many practical jokes.

One time Miller called John Montgomery, who was the director for the tournament we were playing that week, to make sure there would be a courtesy car available for him. Montgomery assured him there would be, and when Miller came to pick up his car, the valet brought him a souped-up low-rider with a four-speed and dice on the rearview mirror. Muttering to himself, Miller squeezed into the driver's seat and proceeded to bounce out of the parking lot, grinding gears the whole way.

At the same event, Montgomery had some of the Tour officials hide a walkie-talkie in a bush just behind Miller on the

> There were many veterans who took young players under their wings when they joined the Tour.

practice tee. About every third shot a voice would blurt out, "Miller, your right elbow is flying," which was one of the idiosyncrasies of his swing that made it so memorable. He would look around quickly and ask players practicing around him if they were hearing anything. We were all in on it, and of course, we said no. This went on for quite a while, until Miller got so frustrated that he picked up his clubs and walked away mumbling something about hearing strange voices. Despite the fun we had at his expense, Miller never lost his sense of humor. When he passed away in 2013, we all lost a good friend and a real a character. We all miss him.

Don January was, and still is, an awesome player. After a successful career on the Tour, Don retired from competitive golf in his 40s to build golf courses. Unfortunately, the economy went south and the market for new golf courses dried up. Undeterred, Don returned to the Tour and won twice during his comeback.

The best of friends, Don and Miller Barber were inseparable and always entertaining. Don was often the instigator in plotting the pranks that were directed at Miller. Don was also a very good friend of Ben Hogan, who shared invaluable information about the golf swing with Don, swearing him to secrecy. Later, in my Champions Tour career, Don and I would discuss this information, as he knew that Hogan had also shared it with me. Since we were both sworn to secrecy, in keeping with Hogan's wishes, that information shall remain private. This is a promise I intend to keep.

Don January is now over 80 years old and still has one of the longest, smoothest, and most powerful swings in the game, especially for someone his age. He is truly a player and shotmaker.

These two friends dominated the early years of the Senior Tour. Don was the leading money winner for three of the first five years. Miller won the money title the other two years.

Learning from a Master

My first off-season was spent traveling between Houston and Fort Worth. After a respectable rookie year, I'd gained some knowledge and experience but no victories. In compliance with Hogan's advice, I'd made detailed notes on all the courses I'd played, and I thought I had a good idea of which ones best fit my game. When I went to Fort Worth and shared these thoughts with Mr. Hogan, he was pleased and asked me which courses I preferred.

As I handed him my list, he lit a cigarette and reviewed it for a very long time. He then put the list on his desk and looked up and stared at me, again, for a very long time. If you have ever been the recipient of a Hogan stare, you never forget it. His eyes would bore right through you. Finally, to my relief, he spoke. He told me that my list was too short and that I seemed to favor only the places where I scored the best. He said that was not unusual, but I had to understand that one year on Tour gives a person limited insight. So frankly, it was too soon to know what courses would best suit my game. He applauded my effort but told me to give the process more time. He told me to keep on charting the golf courses, as that would help for a long time. He then asked if I would like to have lunch at Shady Oaks and then hit some balls and play. Absolutely! Shady Oaks was where Hogan played and practiced in Fort Worth.

After lunch we hit balls in an open area within the confines of the course, away from any would-be spectators. We both had caddies and full bags of practice balls. The caddies went out about 75 yards at first, working farther back incrementally as we hit longer shots. In those days you actually used your caddie as a target when you practiced. It was the first time I'd been to Shady Oaks and the first time I'd actually gotten to hit practice balls next to Mr. Hogan. His caddie didn't have to move much to pick up his shots. My caddie was scrambling all over the place to retrieve mine.

I spent more time watching Hogan than I did practicing. He even allowed me to take some pictures, something he rarely permitted. He was "on" that day and in a very good mood, so I decided to take advantage of the situation. When he started hitting his driver, I asked him what he did to get an extra 30 yards when he needed it. He smiled and said, "You mean like this?" He swung and the ball leapt off the face of his club. His caddie, who was expecting to just reach down and pick up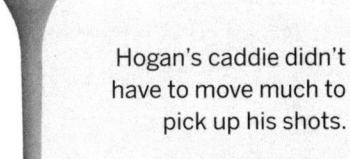

Hogan's caddie didn't have to move much to pick up his shots.

another ball, was startled as the ball sailed over his head. As the caddie ran to chase it down, Hogan looked at me and said, "I'll share that one with you at another time." He grinned then said, "Let's go play some golf." To my disappointment, he never did share how he got to that extra gear.

Shady Oaks was unfamiliar territory for me and played hard that day, with swirling winds. Mr. Hogan watched me closely. Occasionally, he would make a comment or throw down another ball, suggesting a different type of shot. It was a terrific day, but time just flew by and before I knew it, it was over. In the clubhouse he asked me if I needed anything from the factory. I replied that I wouldn't mind having Gene check my irons. He said to meet him there at 10:00 the next morning.

Generosity

When I arrived in his office, he stood up and went directly across the room to a large closet that faced his desk. He slid open the louvered doors and selected three of his personal drivers from a cluster of clubs he had stored there. Handing them to me he said, "Give these a try. They have a special fiber insert that should give you some added distance." He turned to go back to his desk, thought for a second, and went back to the closet. He rummaged through the remaining clubs and brought out a 3-wood with a similar fiber insert, saying, "You need a hot 3-wood and this one should fit the bill. Now bring your irons in and we'll have Gene give them the once-over."

We chatted for a while and Gene returned with my irons. Hogan gave them a quick look and then gave them to me along with the woods. He asked Gene if he'd had to realign any of the irons. Gene said he'd only had to do minor adjustments to a few. Hogan nodded and said, "That should do it. Let me know how they work out." I was dismissed. I thanked them both and left the office. On the drive back to Houston, I thought what a great individual Mr. Hogan was to actually give me some of his own clubs. He had obviously given a lot of thought to what he had observed in my game. I couldn't wait to hit the new weapons.

> "You need a hot 3-wood and this one should fit the bill."
>
> —Ben Hogan

The next morning I was on the practice tee bright and early at Champions. Normally when I practiced, I would start with short irons and work my way up to the longer clubs. That day I was so eager to get to the new woods that I raced through the irons in record time. Now I was ready for the test. The first shot I hit with the 3-wood was incredible. It felt so solid and the ball flight was perfect. I'd never hit a 3-wood that far in my life. The fiber insert was much livelier than conventional inserts made from hardened plastic. That club became a permanent fixture in my bag for many years. The drivers were just as solid and enabled me to pick up some much-needed distance. After hitting all three, I chose the one I hit the best to take on the Tour. The other two would be backups.

It's a funny thing about golf clubs: once I had a 2-iron that was so solid I actually hit it farther than Hogan's 3-wood. One year I was paired with my friend Leonard Thompson in the Chrysler Team Championship. On one par-5 hole, we were preparing to hit our second shots and I asked Leonard what he thought I should hit. He replied, "Either a hard 3-wood or a soft 2-iron." Sometimes, you find a club with all of the essential elements: shaft, weight, and flex matching up so well that you get something extra you didn't expect.

After the practice session with the new woods, I moved on to the Cypress Creek course with the intention of playing 18 holes. After nine holes, I just had to call Mr. Hogan and tell him what a difference his woods had made. He sensed the excitement in my voice, and I could just imagine the grin spreading across his face as he said, "I'm delighted that they worked out for you. I felt they would give you a little extra something. As you get more accustomed to them, you'll be able to be more aggressive when you need it."

Time was fast approaching to start the Tour again. Mr. Hogan and I had several more conversations. I practiced and played every day that weather permitted. Everything was taking shape. I was anxious to begin my second campaign.

Practice with a Purpose

One important thing that I learned in those practice sessions with Ben Hogan was to visualize all different types of golf shots. The idea is that you never want to hit a difficult shot for the first time during a tournament.

Hogan taught me that a golfer must learn to be able to produce a multitude of shots on demand in order to become a true player and artist of the game. This may sound extreme, but Ben Hogan did not settle for mediocrity.

Here again, I learned another distinction between a golfer and a player. Players don't just pound balls on the driving range—they always practice with a purpose. For example, players will pick out a target and then hit an assortment of shots to that target: right to left, left to right, high shots, and low shots. Hitting to a target will provide the necessary feedback to determine whether the shot is working.

> Becoming a player, rather than a golfer, is practicing your shots until you're confident that you can hit any of them.

I learned to practice these shots until I developed the confidence to hit any one of them in any situation. If I wasn't comfortable with a particular shot, I would practice it until I acquired an acceptable level of confidence. Knowing I could hit different shots on demand removed any doubt when I would face a similar shot on the golf course. I was free to think about the result of the shot rather than worry about where the ball would go if I missed it.

As I see it, there is a significant difference between ball striking and shotmaking. A ball striker has the ability to hit a majority of fairways and greens, which he can do with a one-dimensional game (draw or fade).

But shotmaking is more precise. A shotmaker can use a variety of shots and trajectories to attack difficult hole locations. Ben Hogan was the greatest shotmaker I ever saw. Watching him work a golf ball was like watching an artist paint a picture. His canvas was the golf course.

Another difference between ball striking and shotmaking is learning to visualize a shot and then execute the shot as visualized. This became the goal of my practice sessions.

Ben Hogan once said that during a tournament, he always played 18 holes on the driving range before his round even started—visualizing each shot he would play during the round. He practiced until he was satisfied with the outcome, which gave him the confidence to hit the correct shots when the real round began.

The goal in building your game is getting to that point where you see a shot and hit it. Eliminate anticipation. When you stand over a shot, you know exactly where it's going to go.

Becoming a player, rather than a golfer, is practicing your shots until you're confident that you can hit any of them. Then you take those shots to the golf course and use them in pressure situations.

CHAPTER 6

THE 1970s: ON TOUR

In January 1973, I made the journey to California to join the Tour. Being fully exempt really helped both my planning and my confidence. My game had improved, and through the first eleven tournaments, I was able to finish in the top ten five times.

An Incredible Legend

The 1973 Greater Greensboro Open was played at Sedgefield Country Club. It was a memorable tournament for me as it was the first time I met and played with Sam Snead. This is where Sam had first referred to me as Hogan's boy. Sam played great, and after every good shot, he would look over to me and say, "Hogan could never do that." Sam was 61 years old at the time and opened the tournament with rounds of 66 and 67. He ended up 10-under-par for the tournament and finished 12th.

That was the only time I actually played with Snead, although I did participate in a fundraiser with him and his nephew, J.C., years later in Miami Springs, Florida. The three of us participated in a

J.C, Snead, Sam Snead, and me
in Miami Springs, 2002

clinic that Sam hosted for attendees. As the clinic progressed, J.C. and I stepped aside and watched and listened as Sam hit one called shot after another. He was well into his 80s but still so supple and flexible. On the way to Miami, he had actually demonstrated his phenomenal flexibility by standing flat-footed and kicking the ceiling of the airplane. He probably did this more to impress our ladies than to impress us, but for an 80-year-old, his flexibility was amazing. His golf swing during the clinic was still one of the most beautiful and repetitive I've ever seen. We were all in awe. What a great memory!

In 1973, I played a full schedule so I could compete in the tournaments I missed the previous year. This plan would give me a better idea of the courses I really liked and that I would plan to play the following years. I called Hogan periodically to report on my progress. On one of these calls, he expressed concern that I might be spreading myself a bit too thin by playing such a heavy schedule. He suggested that I take a break from time to time in order to refocus. I took his advice and took a few weeks off prior to a four-in-a-row stretch at the end of the season.

My first Tour win at the
1973 Sahara Invitational in Las Vegas

His counseling paid off. I arrived refreshed in Napa, California, for the Kaiser International, and finished fourth. The following week in Las Vegas at the Sahara Invitational, it all came together. I opened with three rounds under 70 and started the final round with the lead. Although Dave Eichelberger mounted a charge and shot 64, I continued playing great. On the tee at the par-5 18th hole, I had a three-shot lead and just needed to make par for my first win.

One thing that Mr. Hogan had always stressed was having a go-to shot to use in any pressure situation. My go-to shot off the tee was a fade, and that day I split the fairway with it, knocked the ball on the green with my third shot, and two-putted for my first PGA Tour victory. Mr. Hogan was as excited as I was when I phoned him. You would have thought he had won the tournament. "I had confidence that you could win," he said. "All your hard work is starting to pay off, and you're learning more about how to play golf. Well done. Enjoy your victory. You earned it."

Learning by Observing

During my career, I had the opportunity to play many competitive rounds with Jack Nicklaus, including several major championships. The first time I played with Jack Nicklaus was in 1973 at the American Golf Classic, a forerunner of the NEC World Series of Golf, at Firestone Country Club in Akron, Ohio. When Jack walked onto the first tee that day, I introduced myself and remarked that he must be scared to death playing with me today. Nicklaus just laughed and played first.

Jack hit a 3-wood off the tee and pulled it into the fairway bunker on the left. I stepped up and striped my drive right down the middle of the fairway. Walking down the fairway I thought things were looking pretty good. Jack then proceeded to hit his long shot out of the sand to about 3 feet for birdie. I three-putted from 15 feet. Fortunately, I recovered, and we both finished tied for ninth behind a red-hot Bruce Crampton.

> Mr. Hogan stressed you should have a go-to shot to use in any pressure situation.

Over the years, I noticed Nicklaus didn't always use a driver on some very lengthy and demanding holes. In one such instance, as we were walking off of a tee box, I looked at his club and saw he had driven the ball with a 1-iron. He caught the glance and smiled. After the round he asked me to remain in the scoring area. When he finished checking his card, he explained why he chose a 1-iron for that tee shot. That particular hole was visually awkward for him, and he just didn't feel comfortable with driver. He used the 1-iron to keep the ball in the fairway, figuring that if he made four pars on that hole for the week, he would be better off than the rest of the field.

This strict commitment to course management reminded me a lot of what Ben Hogan had always stressed to me: play to your strengths and form a plan for each venue. Nicklaus played within himself, under control, with a game plan from which he did not deviate. He had the mental strength to stay within his game plan regardless of the circumstances. If the world were spinning out of control, Jack would see everything in slow motion. He was that focused.

Unlike Palmer, who seemed to play all the time, Nicklaus played a more limited schedule. He felt it gave him more time with his family, plus he was always fresh when he played a tournament.

Jack's methodical approach to each tournament almost created an aura of invincibility. He was always a presence and seemed to hang around long enough to give you a chance to beat yourself. Someone once said Jack knew that he was going to beat you, you knew that he was going to beat you, and he knew that you knew that he was going to beat you. It's almost as if he had a two-shot lead before the tournament even began.

> Nicklaus played within himself, under control, with a game plan from which he did not deviate.

In 1973, I made the cut in 3 of the 36 tournaments I played in and finished 12th on the money list, which got me to full exemption for the next season. Since I won a tournament, I was qualified for the Masters the following April. Since Mr. Hogan had retired from competitive golf, there would be no individual practice rounds with him at Augusta. This was unfortunate, as he had a wonderful record in the Masters. Nevertheless, he provided me with his comprehensive notes for each hole at Augusta National.

Throughout 1974, I continued to improve and become more consistent. Although I didn't win a tournament that year, I did finish second three times and only missed one cut.

That year I was in contention at the Tournament of Champions at La Costa Country Club in Carlsbad, California, and was paired in the final round with Jack Nicklaus. On the 72nd hole, my second shot rolled to the edge of the green, where the ball rested against the fringe. On my first putt, the head of my putter got hung up in the fringe and I left the putt 15 feet short. I missed that 15-footer and lost the tournament by one stroke to Johnny Miller.

Afterward, Lee Trevino asked me to meet him on the putting green. He then showed me how to play that shot using a sand wedge instead of a putter, intentionally blading the ball using a putting stroke. This technique eliminated the chance of getting the putter blade caught in the higher fringe grass. Over the years, I've either holed a number of such shots using this technique or, at worst, gotten the ball close enough to the hole to save a stroke.

Someone once said that free advice is worth what you pay for it. I respectfully disagree. The advice I've received from legendary players over the years is more like priceless. It's no big secret that it pays to pay attention and listen to the players who've been there and prospered with tried-and-true methods of making shots. These are proven methods that hold up under the extreme pressures of trying to win tournaments and major championships. You can't put a value on free advice that works.

> Someone once said that free advice is worth what you pay for it. I respectfully disagree.

Over the years Trevino gave me a few more tips for playing shots from just off the green. One of the things Lee taught me is that you can use a hybrid or fairway wood for shots from the fringe. The added loft of these clubs will get the ball on top of the grass and allow it to roll more smoothly, like a putt, preventing it from bouncing around in the fringe and losing speed.

Shotmakers

When Johnny Miller won the '74 La Costa, he was on a tear. At the peak of his career, Johnny Miller hit the ball straighter and closer to the hole with amazingly more frequency than anyone I've seen before or since.

Johnny started 1975 with two consecutive victories and won three of the first four events. The second tournament of the year was in Tucson, and Johnny won by a significant margin. I remember that one very well, because I started the final round three shots out of the lead and shot 67. Under normal circumstances, that would probably be good enough to win, but these were not normal circumstances. Johnny was in the zone and beat me by a mere nine shots after blistering the course with a magnificent 61. I was playing in the group in front of Johnny and birdied five out of the first eight holes. When I checked the leaderboard at the ninth green, I couldn't believe it. I'd actually lost ground. When Johnny made eagle at the 11th to answer my birdie, it was pretty much over and the rest of us were playing for second place.

> "When I won in Tucson in 1975, I'd say the average iron shot I hit that week was no more than two feet off line."
> —Johnny Miller

Later, Johnny said, "When I won in Tucson by nine shots in 1975, I'd say the average iron shot I hit that week was no more than two feet off line. It was unbelievable. When I was at my peak, I would go into streaks when I felt I could knock down the pin from anywhere with my irons. I played some golf that I think is unequaled." Man, what a talent! The week before at Phoenix, he won by 14 and had a 61 in the second round. In those days, when Johnny Miller was on, he was unbeatable.

The King

The first round of golf I played with Arnold Palmer was in 1974, at the Greater Jacksonville Open at Deerwood Country Club. I was still in awe of him, just like the first time I saw him in San Antonio so many years before. He was the King and always will be.

Arnold was someone I truly admired from the first time I saw him on television, charging from behind to win with daredevil shots and putts that flew into the hole.

Arnold was a mentor to almost everyone who came onto the Tour after him. He truly got it when it came to understanding a professional golfer's obligation as a role model, whether we liked it or not. One thing Arnold told me early on in my career was to sign your name so people could read your signature. Arnold always did this and his distinctive, legible signature became a trademark. This was also the case with Jack Nicklaus and Ben Hogan. When many of today's stars quickly scribble their name, the result looks like a Rorschach test. One wonders if fans will be able to identify the player a week after getting an autograph.

Arnold also learned the value of marketing himself off the golf course.

When he teamed up with Mark McCormack, they basically invented sports marketing. McCormack was a lawyer who founded International Management Group (IMG). After breaking ground with Arnold as his first client, McCormack signed Jack Nicklaus, Gary Player, and a host of other sports stars and celebrities. IMG became the benchmark for sports management companies.

Professional golf is a tough game. Every week, all players start at zero and play for a share of the purse. If you miss the cut you go C.O.D. that week, but you still have to pay your expenses. If you make the cut but finish down the leaderboard, you may barely make enough to cover that week's expenses.

Arnold taught us to establish an edge by having outside sources of income so that we wouldn't starve if we had a bad week. He used golf to develop a network of contacts that reaped dividends. He did it by signing a million autographs, shaking countless hands, and being one of the best pro-am partners you could imagine.

That's how Arnold sold himself and also how he sold professional golf. Because of Arnold, the appeal of golf grew beyond people who played the game. Because of Arnold, more money was infused into the system, allowing

> Because of Arnold, almost everyone who earned a PGA Tour Card had the opportunity to make a comfortable living.

almost everyone who earned a PGA Tour Card the opportunity to make a comfortable living. When Arnold turned professional in 1954, the total available prize money for that year was $600,819. By 1970, that amount had increased more than tenfold.

Someone once said every player should send a portion of every check they win to Arnold. I doubt if Arnold needs any monetary assistance these days, but he definitely has his fingerprints on every one of those dollars.

I was fortunate to be part of two milestones in Arnold's career.

In 1994, the US Open was held at Oakmont Country Club in Pittsburgh. Arnold was 65 at the time, and he had announced that this would be his last US Open. It was a fitting finale since Oakmont was in the middle of Palmer Country. Luckily, I was part of Arnold's threesome for the first two rounds, along with Rocco Mediate. The galleries that followed us for the first two rounds were massive—Arnie's Army came out in force to be a part of their leader's final US Open.

As we made our way to the 18th hole on the second day, it was obvious Arnold wasn't going to make the cut. However, he put his second shot onto the green, about 25 feet from the hole.

As we approached the green, the noise was deafening. Rocco and I stayed well back to show our respect and allow Arnold to take the spotlight he so rightfully deserved. After he reached the green, Arnold turned and motioned to Rocco and me to join him. He then leaned into us and said, "You guys go ahead and putt out, because these folks are going to go nuts when I drain this son of a gun."

Lee Trevino, Arnold Palmer, and me
2006 Administaff Small Business Classic (now the Insperity Invitational)

Needless to say, the crowd did indeed go nuts when Arnold Palmer ended his US Open career by making that 25-footer. His putt flew into the hole like the Palmer of old, thrilling the crowd and bringing them to their feet with thunderous applause. I still get goose bumps when I remember that day.

Arnold's last competitive round of golf was played on the Champions Tour during the 2006 Administaff Small Business Classic (now called the Insperity Invitational) at Augusta Pines Golf Club in Houston. Again, I was fortunate to be part of Arnold's threesome, which included Lee Trevino. After the round, Arnold signed his golf ball and gave it to Trevino. He then signed his glove and gave it to me. I keep that glove locked away for safekeeping, a memento not only of a great day but also of one of golf's greatest icons.

The 1975 and 1976 US Opens

After that first win in Las Vegas, I became pretty caught up in myself. I was having way too much fun and forgot the work commitment that had gotten me there in the first place. I thought winning again would come easily and quickly. Wrong! Even though I came close many times in the next several years, it seemed like I always found a way to lose.

The 1975 season started out great, with six top-ten finishes in the first ten tournaments of the year. For the rest of the year, I kept knocking at the door with four more runners-up spots and ended the year eighth on the money list. The biggest highlight and biggest disappointment both happened at Medinah Country Club in Chicago, during the US Open.

Tom Watson opened the 75th playing of the US Open with blistering rounds of 67 and 68, setting a 36-hole scoring record. Tom ran into trouble over the weekend, and Frank Beard ended up leading by three shots with 18 holes to play. I'd been playing steady all week, but I couldn't buy a putt. On the 14th hole of the final round, I drained a 40-footer that brought me back to even par for the day. After making par on the remaining holes, I finished the tournament at 3-under-par and was the leader in the clubhouse with one group still on the course. Lou Graham had a one-shot lead on the 18th tee, but he hit his approach shot into the greenside bunker. When he failed to get up and down, we ended up tied for the lead.

Lou Graham and me at the 1975 US Open

Lou and I squared off in an 18-hole playoff on Monday, where he beat me by two strokes. From tee to green I again played well but couldn't buy a putt. I hit 16 greens in regulation that day but could not register a single birdie. Lou putted beautifully and walked away with the trophy. I was devastated to come so close and not win. That empty feeling is something that never really goes away—it's always there in the back of your mind and in your dreams.

Lou's wife, Patsy, was so kind and tried to soften the blow at the trophy presentation. She whispered in my ear, "I'm so sorry, but please understand that this might have been my husband's last chance to win the US Open. You're young and talented and will have many more opportunities, and we wish you only the best." Now that was class!

That story repeated itself the following year at the 1976 US Open, at the Atlanta Athletic Club. I led the tournament after both the second and third rounds. I was hoping that my misfortune at Medinah might turn into good fortune in Georgia and make Patsy Graham a clairvoyant.

In the final round, Jerry Pate mounted a charge and birdied the 15th hole, cutting my lead to one shot. After I bogeyed the 16th, we were tied for the lead. We both hit the green with our tee shots on the par-3 17th. Knowing I needed to make a birdie to win, I was too bold with my birdie putt and the ball ran well past the hole. I missed the par putt and now trailed Pate by one stroke. On the final hole, I drove my ball into the rough and was faced with a difficult shot from a bad lie over the pond that guarded the front of the 18th green.

> If I had that shot to play over, I would have made exactly the same decision.

Although Jerry had also driven into the rough, he had a perfect lie and I knew that my only chance to win would be if I could make a birdie. Unfortunately, my 4-wood approach shot came up short and found the water. Jerry hit his historic 5-iron to within three feet of the hole to win.

I wound up finishing tied for fourth for the championship. Many of my fellow competitors criticized that approach shot, suggesting that it would have been smarter to lay up and play for par, securing either a runner-up spot or third-place finish.

As I look back on it, if I had that shot to play over, I would have made exactly the same decision. I wasn't there to settle for second or third place—my goal was to win the tournament. There was no way to win with just a par, and the only way to make birdie was to get the ball on the green. I wish there had been a better result, but it was the right shot to hit at the time.

Jerry Pate made a comment in a post-tournament interview when asked about my two close calls in back-to-back US Opens. He said something to the effect that as he saw it, I needed to learn how to finish off a golf tournament.

Losing back-to-back US Opens was devastating. Mr. Hogan was supportive, but I wasn't listening. How could I blow the US Open two years in a row? I had nightmares about it. Hogan understood. In one conversation he said something that finally hit home: "Son, you have a choice. You can either let this destroy your career or learn from the experience and become tougher and more determined." Wow! It became a choice. I could either fade away into oblivion or step up and become a part of history. I decided to buckle down. I became more dedicated and reinstated a rigorous work ethic. I put in long hours practicing and continued to play a lengthy schedule.

> "You can either let this destroy your career or learn from the experience and become tougher and more determined."
> —Ben Hogan

Playing Hurt

By the end of July 1976, I began to experience quite a bit of pain in my left wrist, which was eventually diagnosed as severe tendinitis. I tried to play through it, but the constant pain proved to be too much and had a disastrous effect on the last tournaments I played that year. I was advised to rest my wrist in the off-season.

The first tournament in 1977 was the Bob Hope Desert Classic in Palm Springs., California. I hoped this would be the kick-off of a great year. I always loved the desert but my start was horrendous, opening with an 83 and 84. My wrist wasn't much better than before, and I had to withdraw from one of my favorite events. I could only play in 13 tournaments that year and made less than $10,000.

Most of the year was spent healing and rehabilitating my wrist. I was totally dejected and drowning in self-pity. I couldn't understand why this was happening to me. Mr. Hogan was sympathetic to a point, but I was so self-engrossed I didn't understand how he could dismiss my dilemma so easily.

Since I couldn't play golf, I had plenty of time to reflect. It finally dawned on me why Hogan had taken such a nonchalant approach to my situation. How could I have been so stupid? When he was in the prime of his career, Ben Hogan had almost been killed in a head-on collision with a bus. He was driving on a foggy road in West Texas when the bus suddenly appeared in his lane. With the collision imminent, he instinctively threw himself across his wife Valerie to save her. His body was crushed by the impact.

> It finally dawned on me why Hogan had taken such a nonchalant approach to my situation.

Hogan suffered a fractured pelvis, fractured collarbone, fractured ankle, and chipped ribs. In addition, he had severe blood clots in his legs that would plague him the rest of his life. The fact that he even lived was incredible. The experts said he would never play golf again. Of course, Hogan proved both the experts and the doctors wrong. What will and determination it must have taken for him to overcome such obstacles! The pain he must have endured to get back to a level where he could play professional golf is unimaginable. He persevered and played phenomenal golf after the accident.

He never discussed the details of the crash with me. When I thought about his recovery, I better understood the depth of his character. It was time for me to regain some mental sobriety. It was time for me to stop complaining and start focusing. After that, when I spoke to Mr. Hogan, I no longer mentioned my injury. I trained hard, and when I could practice again, I went back to the basics I'd learned from him. I travelled to Fort Worth a few times to talk, practice, and play with Mr. Hogan at Shady Oaks.

When I rejoined the Tour later in 1977, it was almost like starting over. Near the end of the year, it did start to get better. Hogan assured me the physical part of my game would be there—I just needed to be patient, as it would take a few tournaments to regain the mental toughness needed to compete. Boy, was he ever right! I was nervous and filled with self-doubt, but nothing really hurt anymore except my ego. I finished the year making a few cuts, but little else. Hogan urged me to hang in there and said that my work ethic and experience would pay off down the road. I came home from the Tour with a positive game plan for next year.

Because of the injury and my limited play in 1977, I plummeted to 150th on the money list and lost my exempt status on the Tour. It was going to be like starting over again when the 1978 season started. I would have to rely on playing well to stay away from Monday qualifying. For the first half of the year, I had some pretty good moments, including a 3rd at Doral and an 8th at Colonial, but no wins.

Redemption

The 1978 PGA Championship was being played at Oakmont Country Club outside Pittsburgh. Oakmont was a special place, as Ben Hogan had won the US Open there during his remarkable 1953 season. That year, Hogan had entered six tournaments and won five of them, including three major championships: the Masters and both the US and British Opens. He was unable to play in the PGA Championship that year, as the dates overlapped with those of the British Open.

In the opening round at Oakmont, I shot a lackluster 75. Afterward, I hit the driving range, practiced until dark, and felt like I'd found something in my swing that had been missing. During the next three rounds, I played nearly flawless golf, shooting 67 on Friday and following that up with a 68 on Saturday.

> After an opening round of 75, I hit the driving range, practiced until dark, and felt like I'd found something in my swing that had been missing.

Unfortunately, a guy named Tom Watson was also lighting up the golf course. After the third round, I found myself in fifth place, trailing Watson by seven strokes. On Sunday, Watson and I were paired in the final group. I played one of the best rounds of my career and ended up shooting a smooth 66. Tom struggled a bit and finished with a 2-over-par 73. The turning point of the round came at the 10th hole, when I drained a 60-foot bomb for birdie and Tom made a double bogey. After the 15th hole I had a one-shot lead, but I three-putted the 16th and dropped back to tie with Watson. We both made par at the 17th hole and both had birdie putts at 18. Tom left his putt short and I ran mine past the hole. As I walked past Tom to finish off my par, he remarked that at least I gave mine a chance. Tom Watson was always a gentleman, even in the heat of intense competition.

At the end of regulation play, Tom and I finished in a three-way tie for first place with my old nemesis from 1976, Jerry Pate. Pate actually had the chance to win the tournament in regulation, but he missed a three-foot putt for par on the 18th hole.

The three of us headed to the first tee for a sudden-death playoff. We all made par on the first hole. On the second hole, a short but demanding par-4, both Pate and Watson hit irons off the tee for position. I chose a 3-wood to give me a shorter shot into one of Oakmont's most treacherous greens. It was the same 3-wood that Mr. Hogan had given me in his office several years ago. Hitting a 3-wood off the second tee was how I'd played that hole all week, and I wasn't changing my game plan. I striped the 3-wood down the middle of the fairway.

> As soon as I stroked it, I knew the ball was on a good line.

Watson's second shot landed on the green, but he was a long way from the hole. Pate's second shot landed short of the green, and he was facing a challenging up-and-down to save his par. Since I was positioned farther down the fairway, I had a shorter iron to the green. I attacked the flag with a 9-iron, leaving me a 12-foot downhill, side hill, left-to-right birdie putt—one of the fastest putts on the course.

Pate and Watson were both unable to convert their birdie attempts, so now it was up to me. Would I be able to gather my thoughts and get some measure of redemption for failures in previous US Opens? Was Hogan right? Was I tough enough?

The putt was so fast that all I really had to do was get the ball rolling. As soon as I stroked it, I knew the ball was on a good line. Just like it did on that practice green in Kerrville when I was 13 years old, the ball rolled true and disappeared dead center into the hole. I immediately lost my mind, jumped into the air, and ran around the green like a madman. I'd won my second tournament and it was a major championship. Thinking back to Pate's admonition from a few years before, it now appeared that I'd learned how to finish off a tournament.

Mr. Hogan had purposely not called me that week for fear of breaking my concentration and focus. That's what he told me when I phoned him from the clubhouse. He was in the midst of celebrating my victory and was ecstatic. "Young man," he said, "you did it. What a huge step in your career. You have now established yourself as a major champion. You have learned a lot about golf but even more about yourself." I told him how much I appreciated his invaluable advice and that I would be forever indebted to him for his patience and belief in me. The conversation ended with my promise to visit him soon.

The experience of winning a major championship was incredible. The adrenaline rush was such that I barely slept at all the night of my victory, afraid I might wake up and realize it was all just a dream.

The momentum of that victory carried over to the following week at the American Optical tournament in Worcester, Massachusetts. During that tournament, I hit almost every green in regulation and several par-5s in two. Entering the final round, I was tied for second place with Gil Morgan, one shot behind Mark Hayes. My playing partner that day was Raymond Floyd, who

Winning the 1978 PGA Championship

trailed Gil and me by two shots. Raymond and I went head-to-head all day, matching shot for shot. When the dust settled we had both shot 67. My birdie on 17 and par at 18 gave me a two-stroke victory over Raymond and Gil. I'd won two tournaments in a row, including a major.

Ironically, that victory wasn't very popular with the optometry community, as Dr. Gil, who is an optometrist, had just signed an endorsement contract to represent the tournament sponsor.

Winning the PGA Championship gave me a ten-year exemption on the Tour. For the next ten years, I would be able to select the tournaments I wanted to play. It gave me an automatic entry into invitational tournaments and a five-year exemption into the majors. Invitational events have smaller fields that are filled with players who meet specific playing criteria. Entry in those events is more restricted than that of a standard PGA Tour event.

When I arrived back in Houston after those two incredible weeks, I was given a most memorable surprise victory party at Champions Golf Club. It was an incredible evening, with my family and all my Champions friends sharing in the festivities. What a celebration! The next day Houston Mayor

Me and my mother at
John Mahaffey Appreciation Day in Kerrville

Jim McConn presented me with the Key to the City, declaring that day John Mahaffey Day. Talk about being on top of the world!

Then came the cherry on top of the sundae: my hometown hosted John Mahaffey Appreciation Day. Kerrville held a gala dinner in the ballroom at the Inn of the Hills Hotel. Famed ABC Sports broadcaster Chris Schenkel was the master of ceremonies, introducing those who toasted and roasted me. In addition to my family and friends, the legendary Byron Nelson was in attendance. The following day, Byron and Chris hosted a golf outing at Riverhill Country Club as a continuation of the festivities. Byron had fallen in love with the Hill Country, and after he and Joe Finger redesigned the course at Riverhill, both of them acquired homes in that community.

This would be the only time I'd get to play with Mr. Nelson. He was 66 years old at the time and well into retirement. Nevertheless, his rhythm and balance were impeccable, and with each swing, his shots flew straight as an arrow. Byron Nelson was one of the most pleasant men I'd ever been around, and his affability made the event even more special. He and

Schenkel smiled, posed for pictures, and patiently answered questions at each request. Their generosity with their time and talent was overwhelming and greatly appreciated. It was a special day for me, and it was great to be able to share it with my parents.

A New World

Two additional privileges came with my PGA win.

I was selected, along with US Open winner Andy North, to represent the United States in the 1978 World Cup. The

Warming up with Byron Nelson

tournament was played that year in Hawaii, at Princeville on the island of Kauai. Andy and I were unbeatable that week. I won the individual honors and Andy finished second. We finished ahead of an Australian team comprised of Wayne Grady and Greg Norman. It was an unusual week, as many of the teams competing came from countries that had difficulty fielding a two-man team. When Andy and I walked onto the practice tee, many of these guys would stop practicing and would sit and watch us hit balls.

When the World Cup was held in Athens, Greece, the following year, I was selected to play in the event once again. This time my partner was Hale Irwin, and we finished first, ahead of Scotsmen Sandy Lyle and Ken Brown. Talk about contrasts. After playing the previous year in the idyllic paradise of Kauai, the tournament in Athens was held on a golf course that abutted a runway at the international airport. The Glyfada Golf Club was so close to that runway that you could wave to the pilots as they landed—and they would sometimes wave back! Hale Irwin won the individual honors, and I finished in the top five to secure back-to-back World Cup victories for the United States. I was proud to have been a member of both teams.

My play during 1978 certainly made up for the previous year's misfortunes and all of the physical and mental anguish that went along with trying to play while injured. I climbed back to 12th place on the money list and was finally healthy again.

To underscore this comeback, I was the recipient of the 1979 Golf Writers of America Ben Hogan Award for being the Comeback Player of the Year. Having Mr. Hogan's name on an award presented to me was so very special. The ceremony was held at the Rye Hilton near Westchester, New York. At the gala, Chi Chi Rodriguez and I preceded Bob Hope on the stage. For golf outings, I'd developed a routine in which I mimicked Chi Chi's voice and idiosyncrasies. This was the first time that I'd done it in front of Chi Chi, but sensing an opportunity, he fell right into the gag and we had the audience rolling in the aisles. As we walked off-stage, Bob Hope whispered to us that it was never a good idea to upstage the star. I assumed he was just kidding, but judging from the crowd's reaction to our performance, I'm not so sure.

> Having Mr . Hogan's name on an award presented to me was so very special.

Ryder Cup Changes

My strong play that year also earned me a spot on the 1979 Ryder Cup team, which would be played at the Greenbrier in West Virginia. Being selected for that team was one of my greatest honors and somewhat made up for not having a chance to play on the Walker Cup team as an amateur. Prior to 1979, the Ryder Cup pitted the best of the United States against a team from Great Britain and Ireland. That year, the format changed. In an attempt to create a more competitive event, players from all of Europe became eligible to compete. Spaniards Seve Ballesteros and Antonio Garrido joined the European team.

The sides were fairly even in the team matches over the first two days. The Europeans have historically done very well in the four-ball-and-foursomes format. Hale Irwin and I lost to Bernard Gallacher and Brian Barnes on the first day, and Sandy Lyle and Tony Jacklin thrashed Lee Elder and me in the alternate-shot format on Day 2.

The United States held a mere one-point advantage over Europe as we entered the Sunday singles matches. On that day, our team rose to the occasion and blew away the Europeans, winning 8 of the 12 matches. I had a hard-fought singles match with Scotland's Brian Barnes and pulled out a 1-up victory for the United States. It felt great to finally contribute and win a point for my country. My victory ensured that the United States would at least tie and therefore retain the Cup. Hale Irwin's convincing 5 and 3 victory over Des Smyth finished off the Europeans. Larry Nelson was MVP of that Ryder Cup, winning all five of his matches; all of them over Seve Ballesteros, including a 3 and 2 win in singles.

The 1979 Ryder Cup US Team
(Kneeling L-R) John Mahaffey, Larry Nelson, Lanny Wadkins, Fuzzy Zoeller, Hubert Green; (Standing L-R) Tom Kite, Mark Hayes, Lee Elder, Lee Trevino, Capt. Billy Casper, Andy Bean, Hale Irwin, Gil Morgan

Icing on the Cake

After the 1978 season ended, I received an invitation from the Hogan Company to attend a banquet at Shady Oaks during the week of the Colonial tournament. Mr. Hogan now had quite a few players representing his company, and he had implemented a bonus pool based on performance. The banquet was held to honor his players and present them with bonuses.

When Colonial week rolled around that May, all the Hogan players congregated at Shady Oaks for the celebration. We were on the edge of our seats when Mr. Hogan rose to speak. He said he was so proud of the players he had chosen to continue his legacy through their representation of his company on the Tour. He was visibly moved and spoke with conviction and emotion. We hung on his every word. It was obvious that he had taken great care to choose the players whom he felt would best represent him. Mr. Hogan's voice actually cracked, almost tearfully, several times during his speech—indicating his true feelings for all of us. When he concluded, we gave him a huge round of applause and a standing ovation. He seemed overwhelmed and somewhat embarrassed. He sat down and we all had dessert.

Receiving a diamond ring from Ben Hogan

A short while later, Mr. Hogan stood up again and announced it was time for the bonus program awards. It was to become an evening I'd never forget. He presented the bonuses to players in ascending order. He spoke fondly about each player as he gave him his bonus, reflecting on the player's accomplishments from the previous year. I was getting more and more anxious as he worked his way through the roster, player by player, knowing that I would be the last recipient. I'd tried to prepare an acceptance speech, but how could I put into words all that this golfing icon had meant to me? What do you say to your hero?

Finally, the moment arrived. Mr. Hogan called me to the stage to present me with my bonus. To my surprise, not only did he hand me a check, but with a big smile, he handed me a diamond ring he'd had a jeweler design for the occasion. I was speechless. Everything became a blur. I do remember him saying some very kind words, but to this day, I can't remember what they were.

The speech I'd intended to use flew out the window. Instead, I recounted our history from that first meeting at Champions and ended by thanking Mr. Hogan for all his insight and support. My remarks seemed to touch him deeply. He knew. After the festivities, he stayed around for individual pictures with some of us. It was a glorious night, but it was over in the blink of an eye when he left with his wife, Valerie. I'd always known that he was a special person, but I hadn't realized just how special. I drove back to my hotel in a daze, and then I realized it was time to get down to business. After all, there was a tournament to play the next day, and appropriately, it was to be played at Hogan's Alley, Colonial Country Club.

One other fantastic opportunity came along around this time: The Woodlands Golf and Country Club approached me to represent them on the PGA Tour. The Woodlands is a planned community, consisting of golf courses, neighborhoods, and commercial enterprises. It was marketed as "Your new hometown." Over the years, it has grown by leaps and bounds. Located just north of Houston, The Woodlands is a terrific facility for play and practice, and, it's close to George Bush International Airport, making travel in and out very convenient.

The gentleman who hired me, Burt Cabanas, had come to The Woodlands from The Doral in Miami. Along with Burt, I was under the watchful eye of Roger Galadis, who had come to The Woodlands from Friendswood, Texas, and was in charge of managing the whole development.

The Woodlands also possessed challenging golf courses and was selected to host the Shell Houston Open. The tournament was played on the West Course from 1975 through 1984, and then it moved to TPC Woodlands from 1985 to 2002. I moved to The Woodlands in the early 1980s and have maintained a residence there ever since. We enjoyed a wonderful relationship for almost 20 years, until a change of management unfortunately brought it to an end. However, this does illustrate the benefits that come from winning a major.

The euphoria from the end of the 1978 season carried right into the start of 1979. The first tournament of the year was the Bob Hope Chrysler Classic in Palm Springs. I opened the tournament with a 66. On Thursday, I played my second round at LaQuinta and fired another 66, including a run of seven straight birdies. On Sunday, I held the lead and was playing in the last grouping for the final round. Lee Trevino was playing in the group in front of us and was firing on all cylinders. Fortunately, I was able to withstand his charge and made a 14-foot putt for birdie on the final hole, the par-5 18th at Indian Wells Country Club, to edge Trevino by one shot. Lee was watching from behind the green, expecting to be in a playoff. He was in mid-bite of an apple when my putt rolled in. I'm pretty sure he didn't finish that apple.

With this win, coming right after the amazing finish of 1978, 1979 had all the trappings of becoming a breakout year. I was so excited when I called Mr. Hogan, but he took it all in stride. He warned me to not fall into the trap of becoming overconfident. Unfortunately, I didn't just fall into that trap—I dove into it.

Feeling Invincible

After opening the year in such grand fashion, I played very average golf in Phoenix. Determined to put Phoenix aside, I arrived at the Bing Crosby Pro-Am ready to make it two out of three wins to start off the year. My first round was at Pebble Beach, where I birdied three of the first four holes and felt invincible.

> In professional golf, if you get hurt, you don't play. If you don't play, you don't get paid.

On the par-3 fifth hole, my tee shot was tracking right at the flag and I was salivating, anticipating another birdie. Then a sudden gust of wind came up and the ball fell just short and buried itself in the face of the greenside bunker, leaving me a long sand shot from a buried lie. I thought to myself, *No problem— after all, I'm invincible.* The smart shot would have been to take my medicine and just get the ball on the green, but I decided to try to move most of Northern California in an effort to get the ball closer to the hole and make par. That was a really bad idea.

As I made contact with the planet, I heard a loud pop in my left wrist and felt a stinging sensation shoot up my left arm. I initially shrugged it off as just a stinger, and I finished out the tournament. My wrist kept bothering me, but I attributed the pain to the cold weather aggravating an old injury. We were playing in Hawaii the following week, and since it would be hot there, I thought everything would be OK. Wrong!

In the warm weather of Honolulu, my wrist swelled to twice its normal size. I'd damaged the tendons and was advised that the best treatment was to immobilize and rest the wrist. I had to withdraw in Hawaii and sat out the next three months. The rest of that year would again be a building process, but thank goodness not as bad as in 1977. I did start to play better by the end of the year, but after a great start, it was time to regroup again. Obviously, I still had a lot to learn.

This injury illustrates just how uncertain life is for any professional athlete, but especially for a professional golfer. The reality is you're always one injury away from oblivion. Unlike athletes in other sports, there are no guaranteed contracts in golf. If you get hurt, you don't play, and if you don't play, you don't get paid. It is as simple as that.

This fact can be illustrated by the experiences of two players I wish I'd had the opportunity to spend some time with during their prime: Tony Lema and Billy Ray Brown.

Tony Lema was a boyhood idol of mine. He was wonderfully gifted and full of life. When he won a tournament, he would buy champagne for everyone in the press tent—earning him the nickname Champagne Tony. But at the height of his career, in 1966, he was

Me and Billy Ray Brown

tragically taken from us in a plane crash. It was a time when I was still dreaming of being on the Tour, and I was stunned by the suddenness of his death.

Billy Ray Brown had "Can't miss" written all over him after he graduated from the University of Houston. He had won the NCAA Individual Championship as a freshman and was voted All American in each of his four years. He won the Greater Hartford Open in 1991 and the Byron Nelson in 1992. Playing at Colonial the week after winning the Nelson, Billy Ray severely injured his wrist after striking a hidden root while playing a shot from the rough.

That injury led to a series of surgeries and limited playing time. We will never know how good Billy Ray could have been, but in the eyes of his peers at the time, his talent was limitless.

I never had the chance to meet Tony Lema, but I'm most fortunate to work with Billy Ray on an almost weekly basis. Both of these guys certainly fit the mold of many characters whose company I've enjoyed on Tour over the years.

CHAPTER 7

The 1980s: On the Tour

By the beginning the 1980 season, I was playing well again. Of the first 13 tournaments, I had four top-ten finishes. Then I had one of those magical weeks at the 1980 Kemper Open.

The venue was the Congressional Country Club in Potomac, Maryland. Mr. Hogan had pretty much left me to my own devices for most of the season. We talked occasionally, and he said he felt like I was progressing and that it was just a matter of time before I won again. Just before the Kemper, I called him to ask if he had any advice about Congressional. He told me to just keep the ball underneath the hole. The greens at Congressional can be treacherous. It's a course where the scores won't be low, so pars will be at a premium. He told me to pick my target carefully on holes where there were blind tee shots. Mr. Hogan told me later that he despised blind tee shots.

Congressional is a long and very demanding course, but I was playing well again and was close to the lead all week. Lee Trevino and I were paired for the last round. As we waited to hit our tee shots on the first tee, Lee complained that he was feeling a bit under the weather, after having been out the night before with some of his old Marine buddies. He didn't look the least bit ill, and when he ripped his tee shot right down the middle of the first fairway, I knew he was fine. I figured he was taking a page out of Walter Hagen's book. It didn't work. We played neck and neck until the last few holes, when Trevino ran into some trouble. I managed to birdie the final two holes for a three-shot win.

Refresher Course

When I called Mr. Hogan and told him his advice on the course had been very beneficial, his reply surprised me. He recalled the time in his office when I showed him a list of golf courses that I thought best suited my game. All those courses were on the short side, with very low winning scores. "Now," he said, "you've won five times. Two were on shorter courses but three were on very long courses. What that tells me is that you can play whatever type of course you face. You need not put limits on your game or yourself. You handled a formidable challenge this week, and you won. You should be proud of yourself."

OK, I never saw that coming. How fortunate was I to have this man on my side! In the ten years that I'd known him, Mr. Hogan had been so generous. He had given freely of himself, his knowledge, and his expertise. His own clubmaker was making my clubs. His company supplied me with clothing, equipment, golf balls, and gloves— almost everything I needed to play. It was great.

> It was clear my relationship with Hogan was that of mentor and apprentice.

Hogan convinced me to use my shotmaking abilities to my advantage. "Why would you practice so hard to develop all types of shots if you're not going to use them?" he would ask. Following his advice, I was beginning to incorporate a wider variety of shots into my game, and it was paying off.

Mr. Hogan and I had a unique relationship. I felt we were close, but other than company functions and a few lunches at Shady Oaks, we'd never had a meal together—and I'd never been invited to his home when I'd been in Fort Worth. It was clear our relationship was that of mentor and apprentice. Perhaps it was difficult for him, due to our differences in age. Perhaps it was because I didn't win as frequently as he felt I should. But the good news was I knew he was in my corner and was there when I needed him.

His remark about golf courses being suited to my game was also so true. A good example is Pleasant Valley in Worcester, Massachusetts. The course is very long, and on paper, should favor longer hitters. However, over the course of my career, I had seven top-ten finishes on that golf course, including a win in 1978.

Favorite Courses

If I had to pick my five favorite golf courses, I couldn't do it. But I could name my top six. In no particular order, they would be Pebble Beach, Harbour Town Golf Links on Hilton Head Island, Chicago Golf Club, TPC Harding Park in San Francisco, Shaughnessy Golf & Country Club in Vancouver, and last but certainly not least, Oakmont Country Club, simply because it's the site of my most significant and celebrated win, the '78 PGA Championship.

Pebble Beach is, well, Pebble Beach. Robert Louis Stevenson called the Monterey Peninsula the greatest meeting of land and sea in the world, and Pebble Beach is right in the heart of it. I find Pebble to be the perfect setting for testing a player's talent, patience, and temperament. Not a particularly long course, Pebble Beach plays right at 7,000 yards. It features a number of holes that run along the cliffs overlooking Carmel Bay.

The seventh hole is a short par-3, playing at just about 100 yards and with the Pacific Ocean as its backdrop. Depending on the wind, the downhill tee shot can be as little as a lob wedge or as much as a low-punch 4-iron. The eighth

> Did I mention the wind almost always blows at Pebble Beach? Good luck.

hole has one of the most challenging second shots of any par-4 in golf. It requires a shot from the ledge of a cliff, over an inlet chasm with ocean waves crashing, to a small sloping green on the edge of the water.

The 14th is the most difficult par-5 on Tour. With a tough green to reach in two, the third shot becomes the most critical and is usually played from inside 100 yards to a tiny green with a huge bunker face staring back at you. Oh, and it's also uphill, so it's semi-blind. Did I mention the wind almost always blows at Pebble? Good luck.

The 18th hole at Pebble may be one of the most photographed holes in all of golf. It flows around Stillwater Cove, which runs down the entire left side of the fairway. The Lodge at Pebble Beach sits to the right of the green. This par-5 gem is always a dramatic finishing hole.

Harbour Town is a collaboration of Pete Dye and Jack Nicklaus, incorporating the best of both styles of design. Playing there requires precision and imagination. It's a delight to play, but another relatively short course: Harbour Town's small greens and tight fairways put a premium on shotmaking. The 17th and 18th holes are built right on Calibogue Sound, and the ever-changing conditions there make the two holes extremely challenging, especially on the final day of a tournament.

Chicago Golf Club is an absolute picture of classic design. I played there one summer day many years ago with the great amateur E. Harvie Ward and my good friend Jack Frazee. Even though Harvie beat me like a drum, I had the time of my life. The course just has a great feel about it. One of the most exclusive clubs in the world, completed in 1893, it was the first 18-hole golf course in the United States. Shinnecock actually opened in 1891, but it only had 12 holes at the time. The out-of-bounds rule had its origin at Chicago Golf Club, a wonderful course with a rich history.

Ken Venturi, Johnny Miller, and Michael Allen all honed their skills at Harding Park in their youth.

TPC Harding Park is a course I've never played but have come to know very well while broadcasting the Charles Schwab Cup Championships. TPC Harding Park sits across Lake Merced from the Olympic Club, and it would be difficult to prefer one course to the other. Harding Park was originally designed as a public course and hosted many amateur events early in its history. Ken Venturi, Johnny Miller, and Michael Allen all honed their skills on this city-owned course in their youth. The course eventually fell on hard times due to constraints on municipal budgets and was actually used as a parking lot while the 1998 US Open was being held at the Olympic Club.

In 2000, a movement began to revitalize Harding Park. After a couple of years of discussion and planning, construction finally began. Over a two-year period, the course, clubhouse, and practice areas were brought up to PGA Tour standards. The renewed and improved course has since hosted the WGC American Express Championship and the Presidents Cup on the PGA Tour, and it has twice hosted the season-ending Charles Schwab Cup Championship on the Champions Tour. It's currently known as the TPC Harding Park and is part of the TPC network of courses.

Shaughnessy Golf & Country Club is classic old school—simple and straightforward, with some of the best bunker placements you can find anywhere. Each of the fairway bunkers is strategically located, and the greenside bunkers are fair but difficult. Everything is laid out right in front of you to navigate. The course uses the hilly terrain, the strategic bunkering, and the Fraser River to frame the holes beautifully. The fact that I played on the Canadian Tour before getting my PGA Tour card may have had some nostalgic influence on this choice. Vancouver is one of my favorite Canadian cities, with its water, mountains, and hospitality.

Oakmont, famous for church pew bunkers and lightning-fast greens, will forever remain the most course for me. It was where my whole career changed in one glorious week of the '78 PGA. Playing almost flawless golf for the final 54 holes and earning my first major victory was something I will always remember.

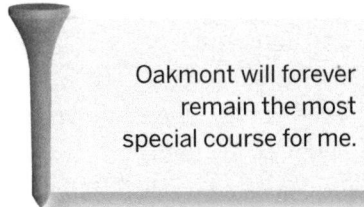

Oakmont will forever remain the most special course for me.

Even though this list is limited to just six golf courses, the truth is that virtually any golf course is idyllic. Each course has its own personality, and like snowflakes, no two are the same. Mountain courses in Arizona vary greatly from the flat courses in Florida. Wooded courses in the Northeast are much different from the windswept links of Scotland. What makes one more favorable than another depends on your game.

Any golf course can be great, and I guess that's the enticing thing about the sport. The reality is that it's not really the course—it's the game and the competition that's part of the game. This game and this competition can be played out on any venue. When you hear that a particular course fits a golfer's game, I wonder if it actually means the player is one-dimensional.

A true shotmaker should be able to take his game to any golf course and adapt to that course. Let's face it; golf courses are pretty much fixed in place, so a player must learn how to score to compete. Of course, you can feel more comfortable on certain courses or even on certain holes if they better suit your eye. Any golfer can play with a more confident attitude when the holes are visually easier to set up on. On the other hand, if the course is visually awkward, it's up to the player to make whatever adaptations are necessary to get the job done. This is why Jack Nicklaus would use a 1-iron off the tee on long par-4 holes that were out of his comfort zone.

After a lifetime of playing golf, and having played just about every great golf course on the planet, there will always be a soft spot in my heart for that simple nine-hole muni back in Kerrville, Texas. On any given day, that course would transform itself into St. Andrews, Augusta, or Pebble Beach, as my friends and I battled it out for yet another major championship. My love affair with golf began on that course, and you always remember your first love.

During my early years on the Tour, I played on all types of courses, and some of them were challenging due to the conditions. Many were described as goat farms, toxic waste dumps, or poor use of a perfectly good cornfield. As I moved along in my career, the quality of golf courses significantly improved as the Tour took steps to ensure tournaments would be contested on well-maintained properties.

After Deane Beman took over as commissioner of the Tour in 1974, he established an agronomy department to better aid golf course superintendents in determining which grasses worked better in different parts of the country. With all the improvements in equipment and the introduction of more hybrid grasses, golf courses not only became more pleasing to the eye but also were kept in better condition, providing more consistent play year-round.

> It's inconceivable to me how anyone who plays golf would fail to follow simple rules of etiquette and course maintenance.

Since the late '70s, practically every course played on the PGA Tour has been in pristine condition. They are well-groomed and usually closed to other golfers for two weeks prior to the beginning of a tournament. When we play on these courses, we're ever conscious about maintaining that pristine condition by carefully repairing ball marks on the green, replacing divots on the fairway, and raking fairway and greenside bunkers. We want to avoid reaching the final round of a tournament and having our chances to win compromised by a ball sitting in a divot.

When I play in outings off the Tour, I'm amazed how members at some country clubs tolerate players who fail to perform basic housekeeping chores. Even though the maintenance staff bears the ultimate responsibility for the condition of a golf course, a sense of respect for the course and fellow players should always be on the mind of every golfer. It's inconceivable to me how anyone who plays golf would fail to follow simple rules of etiquette and course maintenance. Not only would such care result in a better all-around golf course, but it would also reduce maintenance costs for the club and create a more enjoyable experience for all.

The Man from Kansas City

There really was no single dominant player during the 1980s. Tom Watson did emerge as someone to beat, as he won five major championships during this decade. Seve Ballesteros won four majors, and Curtis Strange made history with back-to-back wins at the US Opens in 1988 and 1989.

Prize money continued to grow. In 1980, total prize money on the Tour was about $13 million, and it increased to $41 million by 1989. In 1988, Curtis Strange became the first player to earn more than $1 million in a single season, and by the end of the decade, tournament purses were routinely over $1 million.

The first time Tom Watson and I spent time together was in 1971, at the regional Tour qualifier in Quincy, Illinois. The tournament was held at Quincy Country Club, and both of us qualified to move on to the finals in Palm Beach later in the year. We found we were a lot alike; in fact, we'd both majored in psychology in college. We became friends almost instantly. Tom was a long hitter with a marvelous short game, and that short game would be the key to his Hall of Fame career.

Tom would go on to win 39 times on the PGA Tour, including 8 major championships. He was inducted into the World Golf Hall of Fame in 1988. He also dominated on the Champions Tour, winning 14 times. He was the leading money winner and PGA Player of the year 5 times.

Watson was particularly deadly at the British Open, which he won five times. His classic duel with Jack Nicklaus at the 1977 Open at Turnberry was a match for the ages. Starting the third round one shot behind Roger Maltbie, the pair went at it head-to-head for the next two days, matching each other shot for shot. When the dust settled on Sunday evening, Watson's closing rounds of 65–65 edged Nicklaus's 65–66. With their nearest competitor sitting ten shots back, their "Duel in the Sun" was an unbelievable display of tournament golf. Without a doubt, the 1977 championship would be Watson's most memorable Open—that is, until 2009.

Returning to the site of the Duel in the Sun at age 59, Watson was nothing short of magical. He finished the tournament tied for first and, although he lost the playoff to Stewart Cink, Watson proved to all of us that he was just like vintage wine. He might have lost a step for a moment, but he had truly gotten better with age. He was but a whisker away from his sixth Open Championship. You could say that the old Tom Watson and the young Tom Watson are just as deserving of their place in the history of this great game of golf as are the Morrisses of Scottish golfing lore—especially at the home of golf.

In Palm Beach, Tom and I both qualified and received our cards to join the PGA Tour. As time went by, we became close friends and often traveled to tournaments together along with our wives. We played quite a few practice rounds together and spent a lot of time together when we were away from the Tour.

In Kansas City, locals called Tom Watson, "Fly."

Once I accompanied him on a visit to his hometown of Kansas City. There we shot baskets at the gym where he played basketball in high school, and we laughed as we hoped we'd never end up with 50-year-old bellies. I did, and he didn't.

On that visit, Tom took me out to Kansas City Country Club and introduced me to his teacher—Stan Thirsk, the head professional. Stan was very hospitable and even shared with me the nickname the locals had given Tom. They called him "Fly" because of his constant desire to try to fly his tee shots over all the fairway bunkers at KCCC.

Tom also once came with me to Kerrville, where we went dove hunting with my dad at my Uncle Carl's ranch. The three of us had a friendly contest as to who would get their limit of 12 doves first and with the fewest shots. I don't recall who won, but we were all laughing and having a great time.

We also visited the scenic little nine-hole course where I learned to play, and I pointed out the shallow creek that meandered through the course. This creek was the source of most of my golf balls when I started. It was shallow enough to wade in barefoot and find balls in the soft mud with your toes. This little creek supplied me with plenty of golf balls to use, as well as enough to fill a practice bag. That course was quite a bit different from Tom's country club in Kansas City, but I would never have traded places with him. I loved growing up in my little paradise in the Hill Country.

On one hunting trip, Tom introduced me to quail hunting. He thought I would find it quite different from dove hunting. I guess! I almost had a heart attack when they flushed the first covey. Talk about an adrenaline rush!

> Tom was grumbling about how he didn't get links golf and hoped he could one day figure it out.

Another time we went into Northern Canada to fish for pike. We flew to Winnipeg and took a floatplane to a fishing camp that Tom and his family had patronized for years. The camp had a main lodge for supplies and food, cabins for sleeping, and Indian guides to take us where the fish were. We would get up at sunrise, have a nice breakfast at the lodge, and head out with our guides in small aluminum motorboats on the pristine surrounding lakes. The guides would use the small boats to get us to the more remote areas where the fishing was best. When we encountered shallow spots, they would use paddles until we reached deeper water. The views were spectacular as we floated through crystal clear waters surrounded by breathtaking snowcapped mountains, and the fishing was incredible.

The normal routine was to fish until just after noon. Then the guides would beach the boats on one of the islands that dotted the lakes. There they would build a fire and cook some of the small walleye we'd caught in the morning. After cleaning the fish, they would shake the filets in a plastic bag filled with flour and spices. Then they threw some lard into two iron skillets, fried the fish in one, and cooked potatoes and onions in the other. To this day, those lunches on the islands in Northern Manitoba were some the best I've ever had. Good friends and great times!

Tom Watson had a breakout year in 1975. That was the year he won his first British Open at the Carnoustie Golf Links. We were there together with our wives, staying in a home we'd rented for the week. We went over a week early to get acclimated to both the time difference and the golf course. I was still nursing a wounded psyche after having recently lost the US Open to Lou Graham in Chicago. Tom was grumbling about how he didn't get links golf and hoped he could one day figure it out.

Once the tournament got underway, Watson ended up tied with Jack Newton for the championship and I finished tied for tenth. Tom and Jack were set for an 18-hole playoff the following day.

ABC Sports asked if I'd like to work as a walking commentator for the playoff.

For me, that Monday at Carnoustie was a lot of fun, but for Tom, it was all business. He edged Jack Newton by one stroke to win the Open and become the Champion Golfer of the Year. Tom Watson had arrived, and he stayed. He also seemed to have figured out links golf, as he would go on to win the Claret Jug another four times and was a whisker away from doing it again at nearly 60 years of age.

Dave Marr Jr.

Since I was traveling with Watson, ABC Sports asked if I'd like to work as a walking commentator for the playoff. It would be my first exposure to the broadcast side of golf, and I eagerly accepted. I especially enjoyed the opportunity to work with Dave Marr, who I knew through Champions and Jackie Burke.

Dave was Jackie Burke's cousin and also grew up in Houston. Like Jackie, Dave was the son of a golf professional and grew up around the game. He worked under the legendary Claude Harmon for many years, both at Winged Foot in the summers and at Seminole in the winters.

Marr began to play regularly on the PGA Tour in the early 1960s and won three times, including the 1965 PGA Championship at Laurel Valley in Pennsylvania. He played on the Ryder Cup team in 1965 and was captain of the team in 1981.

In 1972, Dave moved to the broadcast booth, where he would remain a fixture for the rest of his life. His knowledge of the game, coupled with his quick wit, made him one of the most popular golf announcers to ever put on a headset.

Sadly, Dave left us in 1997, at the way-too-young age of 63. His son, David III, is now one of my colleagues on the Golf Channel Champions Tour team.

The Senior Tour Is Born

The Senior Tour kicked off in 1980, under the umbrella of the PGA Tour. It was a direct offshoot of the success of the Legends of Golf Tournament that Jimmy Demaret had started in Austin in 1978. The first year of the Senior Tour, there were 4 tournaments, growing to 7 in 1981 and 11 in 1982. Now the seniors play about 25 tournaments a year.

It was surprising to me that Ben Hogan had not participated in the Legends of Golf, since Jimmy Demaret was one of his best friends. I knew Mr. Hogan still practiced almost daily, and I assumed he was preparing to compete against some of his old rivals. When I asked him if he planned on playing again, his reply both surprised and saddened me. He said that for some time, as he looked down at the golf ball, it appeared to be sitting in a depression, even if it was on a level lie. Because golf was so visual, he felt the adjustment he would have to make in his swing would not allow him to play the game as he knew it. He felt if he could not perform at his top level, it was best not to compete at all. He would continue to practice privately to test new equipment and golf balls, but that was all. It's too bad—he would have been a tremendous addition to the Senior Tour.

I continued to work hard on my game as each year rolled around. Most of the time I played very good golf from tee to green, incorporating the shots I'd learned from Hogan and becoming more comfortable with them. However, my putting was streaky and cost me dearly many times when I was in contention in a tournament. Unfortunately, Mr. Hogan was in the same boat at the time and had no solution for my putting woes. I needed to figure out how to get the ball into the hole more consistently, all by myself.

Frank Urban Zoeller

During the '70s and '80s, as I mentioned earlier, I played many practice rounds with Fuzzy Zoeller and Hubert Green. One of the most genuine gentlemen that I've had the pleasure to call a friend is Frank Urban Zoeller. Fuzzy is the Jimmy Demaret of our era, in that he never meets a stranger. With Fuzzy, what you see on TV is what you get in person. No dual personalities. He also has one of the quickest wits you'll find anywhere.

95

Fuzzy won ten times during his PGA Tour career, including the 1979 Masters and the 1984 US Open at Winged Foot. He also won twice on the Champions Tour and continues to entertain golf fans with his running banter and excellent shotmaking.

Playing practice rounds with Fuzzy and Hubert was always an adventure and usually an exercise in restraint. One time during a practice round, we teed off on a long par-3 hole. We were playing from behind the netting used to protect the teeing areas that would be used during the tournament. My long iron shots normally had a low trajectory, and the 2-iron shot I hit that day actually got caught in the netting. Fuzzy looked at me and said, "Now pards, that's gonna be a tough par."

"You can never do anything again, but you can do something similar."
—Fuzzy Zoeller

During another practice round, on another lengthy par-3 hole, Fuzzy made a hole-in-one. Someone in the gallery said, "Hey, Fuz, can you do that again?" To which Zoeller quickly replied, "No, you can never do anything again, but you can do something similar."

Fuzzy and I took a couple of memorable trips to play in the Philippines Open in Manila. The tournament was played at an appropriately named course called Wack Wack. The greens at Wack Wack had a black, dusty base that mimicked a small explosion every time a shot hit the green. They also had such severe grain that you couldn't hit the ball hard enough into the grain and almost couldn't keep it on the green going down grain. It took some getting used to and reminded me of the common Bermuda greens I grew up playing on in Kerrville.

On our second day in Manila, before we had even played a practice round, a reporter approached us as we sat outside the clubhouse enjoying a libation and asked me how I found the golf course. I replied, "I just walked out of the pro shop, and there it was." Fuzzy almost fell out of his chair. The next question was directed to Fuzzy. The reporter asked him how he was feeling and, not to be outdone, Fuzzy's response was, "With my hands of course." Never a dull moment with Fuzzy Zoeller!

What a Talent

Hubert was more of a prankster. If you teed up a ball and walked away from it, he would either knock it off the tee or pitch it into the crowd—

usually in the direction of an attractive female, daring you to ask her to return it. None of us ever did. If you made a putt on a hole to beat him in a practice round, he would simply retrieve your ball from the hole and throw it into the nearest water hazard. I learned to play my practice rounds with Hubert using old golf balls and made sure I brought plenty with me.

Besides being a prankster, Hubert had one of the most amazing short games I ever saw. He had a great set of hands and could invent shots around the green that would amaze his playing partners. He and Seve Ballesteros each had an incredible imagination and created shots that most players wouldn't even think about, much less attempt in a tournament. Hubert was a fearless competitor who, like Hogan, had a stare that would burn right through you. He was never going to fold and give you a tournament; you had to beat him to win.

> Besides being a prankster, Hubert Green had one of the most amazing short games I ever saw.

In 1974, we were paired together in the final round of the Bob Hope Desert Classic. I was really playing well—I mean almost knocking the flagstick out of the hole on every iron shot. But when I got it close, Hubert got it closer. It was amazing. We fed off each other the whole day, with Hubert coming out on top at the end, shooting 65 to my 69. It was the most fun I ever had playing in a tournament without winning.

Ironically, the tournament where I first met Ben Hogan, the 1971 Houston Champions Invitational, was won that year by a PGA Tour rookie named Hubert Green.

Hubert won 18 more times during his career, including the 1977 US Open at Southern Hills in Tulsa and the 1985 PGA Championship at Cherry Hills in Denver. He was inducted into the World Golf Hall of Fame in 2007.

International Golf

In addition to the tournaments in the Philippines, Fuzzy, Hubert, and I (along with many other PGA Tour pros) had begun to play events in other parts of the world. Japan was always at the top of the list. Asian golf was just gaining traction, and sponsors were actively recruiting Tour players to add some glamour to those events.

In one particular tournament in Miyazaki, Japan, after playing a morning round with Miller Barber, the two of us went to the players' dining room for lunch. There they served a marvelous spaghetti Bolognese, which we both quickly wolfed down. Our Japanese waitress asked in broken English if we wanted some dessert. I ordered vanilla ice cream and Miller ordered the same with an iced tea. Miller had not played well that day and was lamenting his bad luck when the dessert came. I got my ice cream and Miller got an iced tea with two scoops of ice cream in it—an iced tea float. He looked at me and then at the waitress, who stood there beaming from ear to ear. Clearly, she was proud of herself for not questioning his dessert request—although she was probably thinking how weird we Americans were, mixing perfectly good iced tea with perfectly good vanilla ice cream. Miller mumbled under his breath something like, "Well, that's about right. What a day! What's a man to do?" He then smiled back at the waitress and slowly consumed the float so she wouldn't lose face. It was all I could do to keep from bursting out laughing.

On the PGA Tour, winning never comes easy.

At this time, the Japanese economy was booming. Japan had plenty of money but very little space. Golf was catching on in Japan, and many avid Japanese golfers never had the opportunity to play on a golf course. They fed their addiction on countless multitiered driving ranges, because playing on the few golf courses in Japan was prohibitively expensive for an ordinary person. Membership fees at private country clubs drifted close to seven figures.

In order to provide places for Japanese golfers to play, investors from that country started purchasing golf courses in Hawaii and other parts of the United States, most notably Pebble Beach. They then sold vacation packages to their fellow countrymen, as it was actually cheaper for Japanese golfers to fly to Hawaii for a golf vacation than to play on one of their domestic courses.

Back in the Winner's Circle

It took most of 1981 for the putts to start falling. I had some close calls but usually fell just short in the final round. Then in late summer in

Williamsburg, Virginia, my ball striking and putting came together in the same week.

In 1981, the Anheuser-Busch Golf Classic relocated from Silverado Country Club in California to Kingsmill in Williamsburg, Virginia. That year, I finished the tournament at 8-under-par and beat my old World Cup teammate Andy North by two shots, but it wasn't easy. Although I had a six-shot lead with nine holes to play, Andy decided to make it interesting. He really got my attention when he shot a sizzling 29 on the back nine. What had appeared to be a walk in the park now became a tournament again. I'd planned on cruising around the back nine and just focus on making pars, but when I checked the leaderboard and saw what Andy had done, I had to refocus and bear down.

Winning the Anheuser-Busch Golf Classic

When your brain has been on autopilot, that's not the easiest thing to do. However, I made a couple of birdies on the way in and a two-putt par from long distance on the last hole to win by two. On the PGA Tour, winning never comes easy.

The Masters

My best year at the Masters was also 1981, when I finished tied for eighth place behind Tom Watson. Standing on the 16th tee in Sunday's final round, I was in contention and knew that if I could make a few birdies to finish the round, I would have a real chance to win. I hit a solid tee shot on the par-3 16th and solid approach shots to both 17 and 18. All three shots were right on the pin, and all three sailed over the back of the green. Those three bogeys cost me the chance to win the Masters, and I put them down to just being overwhelmed by it all.

Even though I'd faced the pressures of close calls in two US Opens and had won the PGA Championship, I still wasn't able to restrain the excitement of possibly winning the Masters. Time seems to be racing by as your heart beats faster and faster and your mind tries to outrun them both. When things start to fall apart all around you, there seems to be nothing you can do to stop it or even slow it down.

Nevertheless, the experience taught me a valuable lesson in both how adrenalin comes into play and how hard it can be to control during the final stages of a tournament. Even the most seasoned professional at times has difficulty overcoming the overwhelming pressure he places upon himself. Some things are hard to explain and even harder to get under control. You think you've figured everything out just right, and it still doesn't work out the way you planned. Maybe it's like life: you pick yourself up, regroup, and carry on to the next battle.

> The Masters was always a difficult tournament for me.

The Masters was always a difficult tournament for me. The golf course is one of the most amazing spots on Planet Earth, but unfortunately, I had convinced myself early on that Augusta National's design didn't suit my game. I thought I had to drastically change my game to fit the design of the golf course. If I'd been more patient and more confident in my game, I feel I would have played much better there.

Looking back, Ben Hogan had believed enough in my game that he had given me a detailed game plan on how to play Augusta before I went there for my first Masters in 1974. If I'd stuck to his plan that first year, perhaps things would have turned out much differently in later years.

My most glaring act of disregard for his advice occurred that year, during the second round. After shooting 1-under-par on the first day, I was on top of the world and close to the top of the leaderboard. At the start of the second round, I birdied the first two holes and was close to the early lead. Now Hogan's plan emphasized that under no circumstances should I ever hit a driver off the tee at the third hole. This hole is a short par-4, with extremely deep fairway bunkers down the left side. Even with my best drive, I could never carry these bunkers. Since the bunkers are so deep, a tee shot that ended up in the sand could lead to disaster. Using a 3-wood for the tee shot would ensure that your ball was short of trouble while still leaving a short iron into the green.

After the two birdies, I was feeling invincible, so I took out the driver and attempted to play a fade off those left bunkers. The ball didn't fade enough, and of course, it ended up in the bunker close to the front lip. I was furious at myself for breaching the master plan and playing such a reckless shot. I then proceeded to compound one mistake with another and tried to reach the green from the fairway bunker. After leaving two shots in the bunker, I blasted out into the fairway, hit my fifth shot onto the green, two-putted, and made a big, fat triple bogey—7.

My concentration was shot and I was done. I went on to miss the cut after such a great start on the first 20 holes. Later when I spoke with Mr. Hogan, he just asked one question, "You hit a driver off the tee at three, didn't you?" When I answered yes, I could hear the disgust in his voice when he replied, "Yep, I thought so." That was all he said, but I knew that I'd really disappointed him.

I was never the same again at Augusta National. Some nightmares never go away. Every time this one surfaces, I think of the Masters and get a queasy feeling in the pit of my stomach. I played in the Masters 12 times, and even though I didn't have a great record there, I always enjoyed the thrill of driving down Magnolia Lane.

Back in the Desert

In early 1984, I finally broke back into the winner's circle when I won the Bob Hope Classic for the second time. I always enjoyed playing in the desert, and the courses used for the Hope were well suited to my game. Most were tight with small greens, putting more emphasis on accuracy than on length.

I started the final round that year three shots behind Johnny Miller and one shot behind the late Jim Simons, who had fired an amazing 63 during the second round. Firing on all cylinders that day, I shot 66 and was the leader in the clubhouse, sitting on a one-stroke lead over Simons, who was playing in the final group. Jim's approach shot to 18 came up a bit short, and he was facing a 40-foot birdie putt to force a tie. Incredibly, Jim drained the putt and we went to sudden death. Starting on the 10th hole, we both made par. On the next hole, the par-4 11th, I clinched my second Hope victory when Jim just missed a six-foot par putt. Winning is never easy on the PGA Tour, which is why it's so satisfying when you get the chance to hold up a trophy.

The Bob Hope really typified many of the tournaments that were played in that era. There always seemed to be a "name" celebrity—like Bing Crosby, Andy Williams, Glen Campbell, or Sammy Davis Jr.—hosting the tournament. These names would bring their friends to the event, which added a lot of glamour to the week.

The pro-ams at the Hope were a riot. Besides playing with a Tour player, the amateurs would also be paired with a celebrity. I had the pleasure of playing golf with some wonderful entertainers over the years, including Jack Lemmon, Phil Harris, Fred MacMurray, Robert Stack, Glen Campbell, Peter Falk, James Garner, Tom Smothers, all the Gatlin Brothers, Telly Savalas, and many more. One of my greatest thrills in tournament golf was having the opportunity to play with President Ford and Bob Hope on two separate occasions at the Hope. Those two were good friends and golfing buddies, and the barbs flew back and forth all day. It was hilarious. The banter between the celebrities and the pros was always classic and made those pro-am spots treasured opportunities for the amateurs.

THANKS FOR THE MEMORIES!

The 1984
BOB HOPE CLASSIC

Each year in Palm Springs, Bob Hope would also host a reception at his magnificent home overlooking the Coachella Valley. I always looked forward to this event and enjoyed mingling with the stars of stage and screen.

Winning for Mom

1985 was a solid year all around. I finished tenth on the official money list and capped off the year with a win at the Texas Open in San Antonio. That win was special, as Oak Hills was where I had witnessed my first professional golf tournament years before. It also didn't hurt to have a large support group of Kerrville friends and relatives on hand. And, it was the first tournament my mother saw me win in person.

To get that win, I had to birdie three out of the last four holes to tie Jodie Mudd and force a playoff. My mom was so excited and nervous that she stayed in the clubhouse during the playoff. She later said she didn't want to jinx me. After I won the playoff on the second extra hole, she and I talked and laughed on the ride back home to Kerrville. She said that until she saw me play in person, there was no way she could fathom how much a person's emotions fluctuated during a round of golf. "Better you than me," she said, and that was priceless.

Preparation = Performance

The life-changing highlight of the decade came in 1986, at the Tournament Players Championship in Ponte Vedra Beach, Florida. The event had moved to the Stadium Course at TPC Sawgrass in 1982.

The early rounds of the tournament belonged to Larry Mize, who opened with a 66 and 68. On Saturday, I got back into the discussion with a nice 65, but Larry's 66 gave him a five-shot lead going into the final round.

> I slowly and methodically chipped away at Larry's lead in the early going.

On Sunday, I slowly and methodically chipped away at Larry's lead in the early going and finally tied him with a birdie on 16. We both made par on the iconic 17th hole and were tied as we stood on the 18th tee.

The 18th hole at TPC Sawgrass is a demanding par-4 that wraps around a lake from right to left. Throughout the week on this hole, I'd been working my drives from left to right, minimizing the amount of roll and keeping the ball on the fairway. I found it was always preferable to be hitting second shots into this hole from the short grass instead of the rough. Prior to starting the final round, however, I made up my mind that, if I were in contention when I got to the 18th, I would draw the ball around the lake. It would be a riskier shot but one that would leave me with a shorter iron into the green. The downside, however, would be the chance of overcooking the draw and landing the ball in the water.

I stepped up to the ball and hit the drive of my life. Just as I'd envisioned the shot, the ball hooked around the lake, leaving me with a 6-iron to the green. Larry pushed his drive and his long approach shot to the green resulted in a bogey. I knocked the ball on the green and two-putted for par to win.

Winning the Players Championship in 1986

Although that drive wasn't my normal shot, I'd practiced it enough to have the confidence to pull it out of my bag in that situation. And while some writers would call such a shot courageous, courage is a byproduct of confidence. You develop confidence on the range, but you also need to hit those shots on the course. Once you develop confidence that you can hit a shot in any situation, you're no longer afraid to use it in competition. That confidence allows you to be aggressive and make an incredible shot that may result in winning a tournament.

As I said earlier, practice learning to work the ball on the driving range to give yourself a variety of shots to use on the course. It's important to use these shots and develop the confidence that they'll work in a competitive situation.

Think of some of these types of shots over the years. When Tom Watson hit a chip shot from the deep rough on the 17th hole at Pebble Beach to beat

Jack Nicklaus in the 1982 US Open, he knew he could make that shot. He had practiced it and knew exactly how to execute it. Phil Mickelson's shot out of the trees on 13 at the 2010 Masters and Bubba Watson's incredible shot during the playoff for the 2012 Masters are other examples. You simply cannot hit courageous shots in these situations if you haven't hit them before and don't have the confidence that you can hit them again.

Needless to say, you don't learn these shots by planting your ball deep into the Georgia woods. You first learn to work the ball on the driving range, and then practice shaping your shots on the golf course during practice rounds so that when a situation comes up in a tournament, you don't see the lake and you don't see the trees—you see the shot. You confirm that it's exactly the shot to hit in that situation, commit to the shot, and hit it.

Most missed shots are the result of not committing. The lack of commitment, or indecision, plants a seed of doubt in the back of your mind. In pressure situations this seed takes root and usually produces a poor shot. Some describe this as choking, which is more often a result of lack of confidence, lack of commitment, and indecision.

The confidence you develop while practicing will change your entire attitude about pressure shots. Instead of looking for ways to bail out, you'll actually look forward to pressure situations. You'll know you have the ability to hit the shot and will relish the opportunity to execute it.

When Bubba Watson hit out of the trees to win the Masters in 2012, he had no doubt he would put the ball on the green. There was no indecision, no hesitation. He saw the shot, knew it was the correct one, committed to it, and hit it. End of story.

> The confidence you develop while practicing will change your entire attitude about pressure shots.

When Tom Watson sized up his chip shot at Pebble Beach, his longtime caddie Bruce Edwards told him to get it close. Watson famously remarked, "Get it close? Hell, I'm going to sink it." No indecision. Watson knew he could make the shot, committed to it, and won the 1982 US Open.

Probably one of the best examples of a player who commits to a particular shot is Lanny Wadkins. I don't think Lanny ever hit a shot he wasn't totally committed to. (Well, maybe not always on a backhanded tap-in after a missed putt, but other than that, his commitment, confidence, and attitude resulted in 20 wins on the PGA Tour.) That's how I felt on the 18th tee at the Stadium Course in '86. I had no doubt in my mind when I hit that tee shot.

You cannot imagine how satisfying it was to win the Players Championship. It's not called the Golfer's Championship for nothing. Hosted by the PGA Tour, the Players is our championship and the list of winners over the years is impressive. I was proud to add my name to that list, not to mention receiving the ten-year exemption that came with it. I was 38 years old in 1986, which is getting up there for professional athletes. Winning this tournament gave me job security through my 40s and would carry me until I was ready to play on the Senior Tour.

The End of an Era

The 1986 season was a good one. Besides winning the Tournament Players Championship, I had six top-ten finishes and ended the year 13th on the money list. My contract with the Hogan Company was up for renewal and I expected a new multiyear contract and, most assuredly, a raise in my base pay.

Just before the '87 season began, I went to the Hogan factory to discuss my new contract and get some new clubs made. Before I went in to see Mr. Hogan, I first went into the factory to visit with Gene Sheely and get him started on some new clubs for me. When I finally entered Mr. Hogan's office, he introduced me to one of the new executives of the company, who had flown in for the meeting from New York.

> I sensed that I was in trouble when Mr. Hogan explained that the new owners had made some changes.

Mr. Hogan had originally sold his company to American Machine and Foundry (AMF) in 1960. Under the terms of the original deal, he would remain as president of the company and have control of operations and product design. In 1985, AMF sold the company to Minstar. Hogan was 73 years old at the time, and Minstar wanted to have a more active role in the management of the company—which hadn't been an issue for me before the end of 1986, when my contract came up for renewal. Prior to that, all my contracts were worked out between Ben Hogan and me. Mr. Hogan always took care of me and I always did my best to represent and promote the Hogan line of golf equipment. Our normal contract negotiations would normally be concluded very quickly, and we moved on to more important things, like designing clubs or hitting golf balls.

I sensed that I was in trouble when Mr. Hogan explained that the new owners had made some changes and all future contracts would go through a gentleman from New York. Mr. Hogan then shrugged his shoulders, hung his head, and hurriedly excused himself from his own office, leaving me alone with the representative from the new regime. This gentleman then proceeded to inform me that not only was I not getting a raise, but my contract was actually going to be reduced to just a flat salary with no bonus program, all according to the new company policy. Even though I countered that the previous year had been one of my best and that it most certainly had done a lot to promote the company, the man did not budge. He basically said to take it or leave it. I left it.

I went back into the factory and told Gene to forget my new clubs, shook hands with him, and thanked him for all he had done for me over the years. Then I returned to the office to look for Mr. Hogan. Unfortunately, he was nowhere to be found, so I got in my car and drove back to Houston.

> Not only was I not getting a raise, but my contract was actually going to be reduced.

Needless to say, it was an angry ride home. I'd been with the Hogan Company since 1970 and was both angered and saddened at what had just happened. I'd always done my best to represent the Hogan Company wherever I went. In my opinion, their equipment was the best, mainly because Mr. Hogan always had final approval of the products that bore his name. He had been so meticulous in his design and proud of all of the equipment that went out the door. I had been proud to have the Hogan name emblazoned on my golf bag, and I was upset that this longtime relationship had been thrown away so easily.

Mr. Hogan showed little emotion when I last saw him—it was almost as if all he had built was disappearing before his very eyes and there was nothing he could do to stop it. Under the new owners, he became more and more removed from his former duties. Things changed, and sadly, our relationship did as well. The saddest thing for me was that after that day, we never spoke again.

Tour Changes

In 1983, the PGA Tour Policy Board expanded the number of exempt players from 60 to 125. I was against that decision at the time and still am. I always agreed with Ben Hogan, who was against paying too many places in a tournament for fear that such a practice would encourage complacency by taking the emphasis away from winning. At that time, I felt that expanding the number of exempt players to 125 would create an atmosphere of socialized golf, where players would be more concerned with making cuts rather than trying to win. I didn't think the field was deep enough for that number of exempt players. I would rather have had incremental expansions to maintain both the quality and competitiveness of the field. Making an immediate jump to 125 was like the tail wagging the dog: we were setting a field and hoping eventually the quality would come to fill it. Today, I believe it has, but in 1983, it wasn't there.

> Serving on the Policy Board was a way to give back to the game.

During the debate on this issue, I voiced my opinion many times. As a result, in 1986, I was selected to serve as a player representative on the PGA Tour Policy Board. The Policy Board is basically a board of directors for the Tour. Besides the player's representatives, it's comprised of senior staff members and business leaders from around the country. I had the honor to serve on the Board of the PGA Tour for two terms, from 1986 through 1992, and again on the Champions Tour Board from 2001 through 2003. I felt that serving on the Policy Board was a way to give back to the game and help make the Tour better for future generations.

Robert Kirby, former CEO of Westinghouse, was my best source for business information on the Board. During Board meetings, I would almost always sit next to Bob and jot down questions to pass to him about business issues that I didn't fully understand. He loved the game of golf, and his input on the board was straightforward and to the point. No BS!

The 1980s was a boom time for both the Tour and the Policy Board. During my tenure, we introduced a number of landmark initiatives.

Deane Beman was the commissioner of the Tour at the time. He almost singlehandedly moved the Tour from a spare bedroom at his home in Bethesda, Maryland, to the sports juggernaut currently headquartered in Ponte Vedra Beach, Florida.

Beman was born in Washington, D.C., and was a two-time All American golfer at the University of Maryland. He had a stellar amateur career, winning the US Amateur twice and also winning the British Amateur. He played on four Walker Cup teams, where he compiled a record of 7-2-2. Deane turned pro in 1967, at the age of 29, and won four times on the PGA Tour.

After injuries curtailed his competitive career, Deane took on the job of Commissioner of the PGA Tour in 1974—succeeding the original commissioner, Joe Dey, who had held the post for five years. When Beman took over, the PGA Tour had assets totaling about $400,000, and when he retired in 1994, those assets had grown to over $280 million.

Deane Beman made an indelible mark on the sport of golf.

Beman made an indelible mark on the sport. He had the vision to take the Tour into areas that were previously never heard of. I was privileged to witness a lot of this evolution from my seat on the Policy Board.

One initiative of Beman's that has reaped extraordinary benefits is his creation of revenue opportunities beyond tournament fees. One of the major expenses the Tour incurs is the cost of renting a golf course for the two weeks of a tournament. Beman conceived the idea of having the Tour own its own golf courses. This would eliminate the rental fees, plus the courses could generate income all year long. Providing amateurs the opportunity to play on courses where the pros play was one of the key selling points.

The flagship development was TPC Sawgrass, located in Ponte Vedra Beach, Florida. The course was designed to host the Players Championship each year and was the first of what became a network of TPC courses across the country. Pete Dye designed the Stadium Course at Sawgrass, introducing the concept of spectator-friendly golf courses. Now there are over 30 TPC Courses scattered around the country.

Beman also had the vision of establishing a pension plan for Tour players, a revolutionary concept as golf is an individual sport. To accomplish this, Beman tapped the genius of Victor Ganzi, who would later become chairman of the board of the PGA Tour. Victor was instrumental in helping engineer a deferred compensation program based on a player's performance over his career. The resulting program provides a wonderful retirement income for current and former players.

Club Controversy

One issue the Policy Board addressed—or didn't address—was the configuration of the grooves on the face of a golf club. The PGA Tour generally follows the Rules of Golf as defined by the USGA. In the early 1980s, more and more investment cast golf clubs began to surface in a market that had been completely dominated by forged irons. The investment cast clubs were easier to manufacture and also less expensive to purchase. In addition, they had a larger sweet spot, making them easier for an amateur golfer to hit. Because it was difficult to make consistent V-shaped grooves using the investment cast method, in 1981, the USGA made a rule change that allowed a U-shaped or square-type groove.

Ping was the first club manufacturer to introduce this feature, and it became apparent almost immediately that the golf ball behaved differently when struck with a club with square grooves. Shots from lies that in the past had been extremely difficult to stop close to the hole now seemed to stop more quickly. That allowed longer hitters—who had difficulty keeping the ball in the fairway—to still get their second shots

> In 1981 the USGA made a rule change that allowed a U-shaped or square type of groove.

onto the green, effectively removing shotmaking from the equation. The question became whether the player's talent had evolved overnight or whether the groove on the face of the club had created this new phenomenon. With the soft balata golf balls we used back then, the cover of the ball would actually be shredded and you would often find paint in the grooves of the club.

When players complained about shredding, Karsten Solheim, the engineering genius who founded Ping, slightly rounded the edges of the

U-grooves on his clubs to prevent shredding. The design change did reduce shredding, but in the eyes of the USGA, it resulted in a club that didn't conform to the rules. As I understood it, the issue was whether the distance between the grooves should be measured from the wall of the groove or from the edge of the radius. The USGA argued that measuring from the edge of the radius widens the space between the grooves, causing the club to fall outside the conforming specifications. Karsten felt the distance between grooves should be measured from the vertical groove wall, which would result in a conforming club. While the two parties debated the issue, Ping clubs were in USGA limbo.

After passing a ban on square-groove clubs in 1990, the PGA Tour announced it would team with the USGA to determine whether or not these grooves did provide an advantage. They declared it would take a year to quantify whether or not there was an advantage, and if so,

> Players already knew square grooves provide a high spin rate, resulting in higher ball flight and steeper landing angles.

how much. When the announcement was made, Bob Kirby leaned over and asked me what I thought. I told him I thought we would be in the same place next year, with no resolution. He agreed and told Beman. Sure enough, a year later, when the issue came up on the agenda, we looked at each other and said, "Are you going to say it or should I?" I thought Bob deserved the honor, and he seemed to relish the moment.

Solheim sued both the USGA and the PGA Tour. The USGA settled its suit quickly and clarified the specifications. The PGA Tour held out until 1993 and finally adopted the USGA position. Interestingly, the report on whether or not the square grooves provided an advantage was not completed until 2006. It quantified what players already knew: square grooves provide a higher spin rate, resulting in higher ball flight and steeper landing angles. As a result of this study, in 2010, the USGA and the PGA Tour banned square-grooved golf clubs. However, this was not the end of the controversy. A loophole in the ban was created by the 1991 settlement between Ping and the USGA allowing the use of a nonconforming club made prior to 1990. A number of current Tour players use clubs, especially wedges, that are grandfathered in under this loophole.

I went to visit Bob Kirby in Naples, Florida, in the late 1990s. He was very ill, but his face lit up when I walked onto his lanai. We sat and revisited the old days we had shared on the Policy Board. He said how much he missed those days but that most of all, he missed playing the game he loved so much. He was a wonderful man and great friend. He passed away in 1999. I miss him.

In 1989, I was having a very good year financially but had been winless since the Players in 1986, a three-year drought. However, that August I was heading for a city that had been good luck for me ever since my rookie year. That was when I finished second to clinch a spot in the top 60 and earn full exemption on the Tour for the following year.

The FedEx St. Jude Classic was being played at TPC Southwind, just outside Memphis in Germantown, Tennessee. It was the first year we played on that course and I found that with each round I played, the more comfortable I felt. After shooting right around par for the first two rounds, I'd just barely made the cut. So I decided to be ultra-aggressive for the rest of the tournament, as I didn't really have anything to lose. It turned out to be the right approach, as I went on a birdie binge for the weekend. I shot 66 on Saturday and 65 on Sunday to win the tournament by three shots. At age 41, this was to be my final victory on the PGA Tour, but what a way to go out!

That win, coupled with two runner-up finishes, made 1989 the best year of my career financially. I finished 29th on the ever-expanding money list and was playing well and ready to jump into the next decade.

CHAPTER 8

THE 1990s

The 1990s saw another explosion in golf. Although no single player dominated the decade, it is interesting to note that the last major tournament of the decade, the 1999 PGA Championship, was won by a fellow named Tiger Woods. This was Tiger's second major win, following his 1997 Masters title.

The explosion was in the form of prize money. In 1990, the leading money winner on Tour was Greg Norman, who earned $1,200,000 with three victories. In 1999, Tiger was the leading money winner, with $6,600,000 in earnings and eight victories.

Purses grew exponentially. In 1990, the total prize money on the Tour was $46 million. By 1999, that amount had grown to $134 million. The average tournament purse tripled from right at $1 million in 1990 to $2.8 million in 1999.

After my win at the 1989 FedEx St. Jude Classic, my PGA Tour career started to taper off. I had a decent year in 1990, but after that I was struggling to just make cuts. Fortunately, I still had the ten-year exemption that came with winning the Players Championship in 1986. In reality, I was just biding my time until 1998, when I would become eligible for the Senior Tour, now called the Champions Tour.

Deane Beman retired as commissioner of the PGA Tour in 1994, but players on the PGA have benefited and will continue to benefit from his impact on the sport for many years to come. Deane was inducted into the World Golf Hall of Fame in 2000 and received the PGA Tour Lifetime Achievement Award in 2007. Tim Finchem, who was serving as chief operating officer of the Tour, succeeded Beman as commissioner.

Ben Hogan died on July 27, 1997, at the age of 84. In the last few years of his life, he faced a number of health problems, including a bout with colon cancer. Then he had a bad fall that required hospitalization, and he never came home.

I don't recall where I was when I heard that Mr. Hogan had passed away. It had been about ten years since we had spoken, so it took a few days for his death to sink in. As I reminisced about our history, I became very sad. He'd been so kind to me and had put so much of himself and his company into helping me become the best player I could be. After all that support, I felt I'd let him down. I'd led him to believe I had the same driving passion about the game that he had, and at first, I did. But as my career progressed, I allowed other interests and distractions to interfere with golf. During some of the peak years of a blossoming golf career, I made some of the poorest life decisions possible, which drew my focus away from golf. The time I'd previously dedicated to practice was spent in nonproductive activities and relationships. I deceived myself, but most of all, I deceived Ben Hogan. That's something impossible to rationalize or defend. It's something I will forever deeply regret.

> Ben Hogan was the poster child for hard work and his pursuit of perfection is legendary.

Ben Hogan left a legacy that will stand the test of time. He was the poster child for hard work and his pursuit of perfection is legendary. The quest for perfection was the carrot on the stick that drove him in everything he did. He once said, "No one is ever perfect. I tried to perfect it but never did. I came pretty close." To borrow a line from my broadcast colleague, Gary Koch, all things considered, Hogan was definitely better than most.

The year 1998 was a milestone in a number of ways. In May of that year, I both celebrated my 50th birthday and made my debut on the Senior Tour.

Putting had always been the most inconsistent part of my game throughout my career. I was what's usually referred to as a streaky putter. That means if I was on, I made everything. Unfortunately, those occasions were rare, and most of the time, I was below average on the Tour in that category. That's because even though I understood putting was at least half the game, it was just so much more fun to spend practice time hitting drivers and 2-irons, rather than spending the necessary amount of time on the putting green. For years I didn't understand what caused the huge fluctuation in my consistency with the putter. But shortly before joining the Senior Tour, I finally found out.

New Life and Another Shot

Prior to the beginning of my first season on the Over-50 Tour, I was staying with my friend Joe Patterson at the Vintage Club in Palm Desert, California. We were playing 36 holes a day to get me ready for competition. One day we ran into Dave Stockton, who asked me point-blank if I planned on winning on the Senior Tour. I replied of course I did, that was why I was in California practicing.

At that time, Dave was a major force on the Senior Tour, winning and contending with great regularity. He told me that there were several things I needed to understand about that Tour. Since most of the tournaments consisted of only three rounds, they were more sprints than marathons. That meant there was no room for an average score in any round. It was a birdie-fest from the 1st hole to the 54th. So if I was going to be in contention in this format, I had to learn to putt a whole lot better.

I've always had the greatest respect for Dave, both as a person and as one of the best authorities on any Tour when it comes to short-game knowledge and execution, especially putting. When he said he would be happy to give me a few suggestions along the lines of putting, I jumped at the chance. What he said to me changed how I'd thought about putting my entire career and gave me a new level of confidence.

> If I was going to be in contention in the Senior Tour format, I had to learn to putt a whole lot better.

Even though the core information he shared with me is contained in his many books and DVDs, I appreciated his hands-on approach and willingness to share his knowledge.

The thing he stressed to me the most was that I had to establish the same routine on every putt. He explained that while in every other aspect of my game, I had an established routine, in putting, I didn't—and that was a major contributor to my inconsistency. He helped me develop a set routine and made me promise to practice putting at least as much as my long game. He also reminded me I would hit a great many more putts during a round than I would 2-iron shots.

It took a bit of time and discipline, but as I became more familiar with what I was doing, more putts started to find the hole. Once again, repetition instilled confidence. I'd always thought putting was mostly an individual thing and you just went with your own method to wiggle the ball into the hole in pressure situations. Sometimes it worked and sometimes it didn't.

Practice, practice, practice

Thanks to Dave Stockton, I found out it *is* possible to teach old dogs new tricks.

Dave Stockton and Ben Crenshaw are two of the most respected putters in the game, although their styles are very different. If you watch them, however, you will notice they each have a consistent routine they follow on every putt. Coming up with a consistent routine and spending sufficient time on the putting green practicing that routine is what develops great putting skills.

I made my Senior Tour debut in mid-May of 1998. Just as Dave Stockton warned, tournaments on this Tour were flat-out sprints from the 1st hole to the 54th. The good part of this competition was that there were no cuts. Everyone who got into the tournament cashed a check. Fortunately, I wouldn't have to worry about qualifying for many years due to my ranking on the regular PGA Tour career earnings list. However, I quickly found out that playing on this Tour was not as easy as I thought it would be. I would have to work a lot harder if I expected to win.

As I said earlier, the Senior Tour was initially the brainchild of Jimmy Demaret. What started out as a single event at Onion Creek Golf Club in Austin, Texas, grew to almost rival the PGA Tour in number of events each year. Now called the Champions Tour, it has evolved into a tournament sponsor's dream. Each event features a limited field of 78 players and at least two pro-ams, and the players are more than willing to attend numerous functions during the week.

A Champions Tour event is a wonderful vehicle to give a sponsor local, national, and even worldwide exposure. It also gives the sponsor an opportunity to reward its clients, vendors, and employees with prime pro-am pairings and tee times. Players almost always attend functions surrounding the tournaments, such as parties and dinners, giving attendees a chance to converse and rub shoulders with Hall of Fame members, major Championship winners, and multiple tournament winners from all over the world. A Champions Tour event is like Disney World for golf lovers, who can tap into a wealth of knowledge, golf history, and great stories from players who were part of it all.

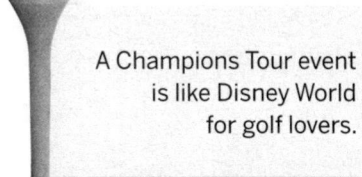

A Champions Tour event is like Disney World for golf lovers.

A Different Look

One company that totally understands the great upside of being a longtime sponsor on the Champions Tour is Insperity. In 1994, Senior Tour golf came to an end in the Houston area. From 1988 through 1994, the Doug Sanders Celebrity Classic had been played at Deerwood Country Club in Northeast Houston. However, the tournament folded amid controversial circumstances after the 1994 event.

Ten years later, in 2004, the tournament was resurrected at Augusta Pines Golf Club north of Houston. I was fortunate to have a hand in bringing the tournament back to my hometown.

At the time, I was representing Augusta Pines on the Senior Tour and was also serving on the Senior Tour Policy Board. In late August of 2002, the owner-designer of Augusta Pines, Dennis Wilkerson, asked if I thought we could host a professional tournament at Augusta Pines. The golf course plays at about 7,100 yards and has plenty of room to accommodate large galleries. It was flat and easy to walk. When I asked Dennis which Tour he had in mind, he said the Senior Tour. I told him that I thought it would be a great idea, and he asked me to help get the ball rolling.

The first thing I did was call the PGA Tour office. The Tour sent Gene Smith, one of the Senior Tour officials, for a site evaluation on October 29, 2002. He found the golf course to be more than satisfactory to host a Senior Tour event.

Dennis also wanted me to help him to select a tournament management company. We asked three groups to provide bids so we could get an idea of projected costs and commitment requirements. In reviewing the bids, we found they all contained the Tour requirement of a three-year commitment. The proposed costs varied slightly among the three companies, but they were so close to each other that Dennis asked, "OK, if it were you putting on this show, which one would you pick?" I didn't hesitate and recommended Pro Links Sports. Dennis agreed, so I got in touch with Hollis Cavner, one of the partners in Pro Links.

It was a great feeling to help bring a tournament back to an area that had been so prominent in Texas golf.

At that time, Pro Links ran numerous tournaments on the Senior Tour and did so in a professional manner, with great attention to detail. Hollis sent Bryan Naugle to Augusta Pines to meet with us. Bryan is also a partner in Pro Links and had been in charge of running the Novell Utah Showdown, which left the Tour in 2001. That left Bryan free to take on another project, and his availability proved to be most advantageous to us at Augusta Pines.

The meetings that followed were all positive, and it soon started to look like getting Houston back on the Senior Tour might actually happen. Dennis agreed to back the tournament for three years, but he was hoping the Pro Links team would be able to secure a title sponsor to help lessen his financial burden. Bryan hired a couple of local semiretired businessmen who loved the game, and he gave them the job of finding corporate sponsors. Lynn Bean was a retired rodeo performer, and Norm Miller was a retired Major League Baseball player who had spent part of his career with the Astros. Both of those guys had lots of contacts in the Houston area, and they began the tedious job of calling on prospects.

One of the companies Norm contacted seemed as though it might have some interest in becoming the title sponsor. Administaff (now Insperity), headquartered in Kingwood northeast of Houston, is a professional employer organization providing human resources services to small- and medium-size businesses. They were interested in increasing their local and national exposure, and a Senior Tour event with Administaff's name on it might fit the bill.

Evidently, Norm Miller knew some of the corporate officers, including Administaff's CEO Paul Sarvadi and Executive VP of Sales and Marketing Jay Mincks. Norm had met them through their mutual interest in the Houston Astros. Norm felt the initial discussions had been positive enough that Bryan Naugle should meet with Paul, Jay, and the other officers of the company. When Bryan met with them Jay reminded Paul they had been down this title sponsor road before and if they didn't do it this time, then frankly he never wanted to hear about it again. But perhaps the thing that put the decision over the top was when Bryan had Arnold Palmer call Paul Sarvadi directly and encourage him to bring the Champion's Tour to Houston. After that, Administaff agreed to become the title sponsor with Pro Links as the tournament manager.

The education I received through that process gave me a whole new perspective on professional golf. As a player, I'd never realized how much work it is just to get a spot on the schedule, much less all the behind-the-scenes machinery necessary to operate a tournament. After a lot of hard work, the Administaff Small Business Classic became a reality in October 2004, and it's still one of the most popular and respected golf tournaments on the Champions Tour.

> The education I received through that process gave me a new perspective on professional golf.

In 2011, Administaff went through a major rebranding process and changed its name to Insperity. Since 2004, the tournament has gone from being the Administaff Small Business Classic to the Insperity Classic, and in 2014, it achieved the designation of the Insperity Invitational. Today, Pro Links and Insperity have achieved one of the most synergistic relationships in professional golf that I've ever been associated with.

It was a great feeling to help bring a tournament back to an area that had been so prominent in Texas golf, and to be part of the creation and evolution of what is now the Insperity Invitational. To this day, I still have a wonderful relationship with both Pro Links and Insperity. It's such a pleasure to deal with gentlemen of integrity and class. The executive officers of Insperity—Paul Sarvadi, Jay Mincks, President Richard Rawson, and COO Steve Arizpe, coupled with co-conspirators Bryan Naugle and Hollis Cavner of Pro Links—are not only business associates but also great friends of mine. For more than a decade, I've had the pleasure of getting to know these gentlemen personally. They love the game of golf, and I've had the good fortune to join them at some of the most incredible golf destinations in the world. I've never enjoyed myself or laughed more in my life than during the times we've spent together.

With its limited field, and with more players turning 50 every day, the Champions Tour is now both the most competitive and the most restrictive Tour in all of professional golf. If a new player is lucky enough to acquire exempt status on this Tour in the first place, he will soon learn how difficult it is to maintain that status. In the past, players in their late 40s had the notion they could simply coast into the Champions Tour when they reached 50. Those days are long gone. Golfers these days have longer careers due to the new emphasis on fitness, so it's not unusual for players over 50 to still be competitive on the regular PGA Tour.

In 1998, my first year on the Champions Tour, I played in 23 tournaments and finished in the top 25 in 11 of them, including a second-place finish at the Utah Showdown. The following year proved to be my best year as a senior golfer, as I played in 32 events and finished in the top ten 13 times. I also won my only Senior Tour event that year in the friendly confines of San Antonio, after a three-way playoff with José María Cañizares and Bruce Fleisher.

CHAPTER 9

NEW MILLENNIUM,
NEW CAREER

The first decade of the new millennium belonged to one person, Eldrick "Tiger" Woods. Tiger owned golf during this decade, more than anyone has ever dominated any sport. Between 2000 and 2009, Tiger played in 252 golf tournaments and won 56 of them—including 12 of the 40 major championships—winning over $80 million in prize money. To put that into perspective, for the ten years from 1972 (my rookie year) to 1981, the total prize money available on the Tour was only around $100 million.

Tigermania has had an incredible influence on golf. Obviously, the major effect was on prize money. Tiger's rookie year was 1996, when the total prize money on Tour was $65 million. Ten years later, the golfers were playing for over $250 million. However, it wasn't all about money. Tiger is a worldwide phenomenon, much like Muhammad Ali

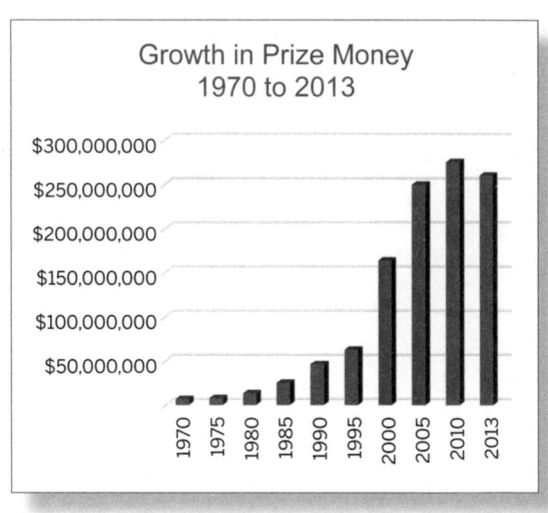

was, and he has brought a multitude of new fans to the game. Many of these new fans have never played a round of golf.

Tiger is a phenomenal golfer. He dominated the sport in the late 1990s and early 2000s the way Nicklaus did in the '60s and '70s and Hogan did in the '50s. Like his predecessors, Tiger's dominance is a combination of a great golf game coupled with intense focus and the ability to intimidate his competitors.

There will always be the discussion of who is the greatest golfer of all time. There's no real answer to this question, only opinion. When you compare them, it's easy to say Nicklaus hit the ball farther than Hogan did and that Tiger hits it farther than Nicklaus did. But it doesn't mean Nicklaus was better than Hogan or Tiger is better than the other two. It simply means each of them was or is the best of his respective era. Each was able to master the equipment of their day, and each had the extraordinary ability to score under pressure.

Hogan's beautiful swing

If Ben Hogan were using today's equipment, he would no doubt be just as dominant as he was in the 1950s. The same would apply to Jack Nicklaus. If Tiger were beamed back into the '50s and given a persimmon driver and a balata golf ball, he would still be a force on the Tour.

What an image it would be if all three of these players competed against each other in the prime of their careers. You would likely see a lot of tournaments like the 1975 Open Championship at Turnberry, when Nicklaus and Tom Watson went head-to-head and shot 65-65 vs. 65-66, beating their next closest competitor by ten shots.

The reality is that the equipment of today has had a dramatic impact on the game. The solid core golf ball can carry 50 yards farther than a balata ball. The result is that today's players are hitting 9-irons and wedges into holes where Nicklaus used a 6-iron and Hogan used a 4-iron. When

Justin Rose hit his 4-iron second shot on the 18th hole of the 2013 US Open at Merion, he was a few feet away from the plaque memorializing a similar shot hit by Ben Hogan in 1953. Hogan used a 2-iron.

The distinction is not just about distance. Overall, players are stronger and more flexible today and the pool of talent on the Tour is much deeper. Scores are definitely lower, but in my opinion, the art of shotmaking has been altered by technology. The game is played much more through the air today than along the ground. I'm not sure if it's better, but it is different.

For the first three years of the 2000s, I played pretty steady golf and had some good results, but no wins. In the first five years on the Champions Tour, I won almost as much prize money as I'd made in 25 years on the PGA Tour. Even at that, I felt my performance was not up to snuff and my opportunities to win were getting fewer and further apart.

After the 2002 season, a number of physical issues caught up with me and my golf suffered accordingly. I was forced to withdraw from three tournaments in 2003 and was becoming very concerned with my overall level of play and increasing lack of ability to hit the shots that had been my bread and butter in the past. It was hard to fathom that I might end my career with only one win on the Champions Tour, but that thought was frequently entering my mind. Not a very positive attitude to bring to the first tee each week. It's never a good idea to doubt your ability, and it's hard to play good golf with that attitude.

Part of the Media

About that time, I had a conversation with Keith Hirshland, who was producing the Farmer's Charity Classic in Ada, Michigan, for Golf Channel. Keith was very straightforward and asked if I would like to give

Interviewing the immortal Seve Ballesteros

broadcasting a try, since my golf game had been less than stellar for a good while. I couldn't argue about his critique of my game, so I called my wife, Elizabeth, to ask her what she thought about Keith's offer. She was all for it. She had been hinting for some time that I should pursue something in television.

The next day I met with Keith at the Golf Channel compound after I completed my morning pro-am round. We chatted for a bit, and then he set me up with a headset, microphone, and clipboard. He selected an afternoon pro-am group for me to follow, gave me instructions on how to operate the equipment, and sent me out for some on-the-job training.

The biggest challenge was conversing coherently about what was happening on the course while someone was talking to me in my headset at the same time. That week was the beginning of what has turned into almost a decade of being able to talk about a sport I love and the players who have been such a major part of my life. I knew Keith and Elizabeth were right. As I finished that tournament 6-over-par and placed 73rd out of 78 players, I knew—it was definitely time for something new.

> As I finished that tournament placing 73rd out of 78 players, I knew it was definitely time for something new.

I cannot thank Keith Hirshland and Golf Channel enough for giving me a chance for this new career. Since my first day on the job in 2003, along with Keith, there have been so many people at Golf Channel who have given me constructive criticism—some in graphic detail—and helped me evolve as a broadcaster. Working with the likes of Phil Blackmar, Billy Ray Brown, Curt Byrum, Donna Caponi-Byrnes, Brandel Chamblee, John DelVecchio, Pete Esposito, Brian Hammons, Brian Hennessey, Bill Kratzert, Jim Kelly, Mark Lye, Joe Martin, Frank Nobilo, Peter Oosterhuis, Philip Parkin, Bob Papa, Karl Schliksbier, and Lanny Wadkins has been a wonderful learning experience on how to do it right and have fun along the way. The producers I've worked with the most—Jack Graham, Keith Hirshland, Jeff Gershengorn, Ray Jacobs, Glenn Savadski, and Brandt Packe—all produce in different ways, but they all are there for me with constructive comments to help me become a better broadcaster. For that I will always be grateful. They have all been most professional and generous in sharing their experience and expertise.

Lanny Wadkins and I have been competitive rivals since we were teenagers. We went head-to-head throughout our college days, with my

Houston Cougars battling his Wake Forest Demon Deacons for the national championship during my junior and senior years. In winning the 1970 individual NCAA Championship, I edged Lanny by one shot. Lanny and I both were part of the 1971 Tour Qualifying School, which was arguably the best class ever. Lanny played in 706 events in his career and made the cut in 489. I played in 704 tournaments and made the cut in 471. We both recorded our first Tour wins at the Sahara Invitational in Las Vegas, Lanny in 1972 and I the following year. We won the PGA Championship in succeeding years, Lanny in 1977 and I in 1978. We also both won the Players Championship. Lanny won a total of 21 tournaments during his Hall of Fame career.

Although our paths crossed many times over the years, I really never got to know Lanny well until he joined our team broadcasting Champions Tour events for Golf Channel. We have since become great friends, and it's a joy to reminisce with him about our careers.

With Lanny Wadkins on the Golf Channel set

Once I asked Lanny how he was able to maintain focus and close out a golf tournament, especially when he had the lead going into the last round. He said he would make up games within the game to keep himself focused. For example, in one tournament he had a nice lead going into the last round. To keep his focus, he set a goal of having no 5s on his scorecard. When he got to the last hole, a par-5, he was leading by 8 shots and surprised people by grinding over a birdie putt. He was more focused on not having a 5 on the scorecard than cruising to a seemingly easy win.

Being able to work at Golf Channel softened the blow of realizing that I'd reached the point in my life where I was simply not able to compete at the highest level and challenge for the lead on Sunday in a professional golf tournament. Now, being part of the Golf Channel broadcast team allows me to continue to be a part of the game I've loved since I was 11 years old, without the frustration of not being able to perform at the standard I set for myself over my career.

Looking down from my perspective in the broadcast booth has given me an even greater appreciation of the skill level of the professional golfer. It also provides a certain level of satisfaction, as I look back at my own career and compare some of the shots I played to similar shots being struck by today's players.

It's easy to criticize an errant shot or a missed putt. From my vantage point, we, as commentators, sometimes forget how easy the game appears from the tower. Golf is in fact a very difficult game that the guys inside the ropes make look like child's play. At times we can make too big a deal out of a player hitting a bad shot. Having been there, I know how hard it is to be perfect on every shot. And also having been there, I realize that no one ever is. Even Ben Hogan conceded that he never achieved perfection.

Early in my career, I had the opportunity to work with the late David

Francis Marr Jr., and I always admired his "to-the-point analysis" of professional golf. A former PGA Champion and Ryder Cup Captain, he had vast experience in the game and a wonderful knack for always giving the player a possible out. An example would be something similar to this: "Obviously, he did not plan on hitting his second shot here, but he has such a marvelous

Dave Marr flanked by his sons Tony (L) and David III (R), my colleague on the Golf Channel

short game; let's see if he can get it up and down for par." Short, sweet, and tells it all.

I happen to relate to Marr's style but also see the need for more critical analysis: sugar and spice. What makes golf such a great sport is that there are many ways to play the game. It's fun at times for us in the booth to disagree with a golfer's decision on how to play a shot. Lanny and I do that frequently because we see things differently. Lanny and I both won on the tour, but we got there differently. He played with a very aggressive style, while I was more conservative. However, I did win my last tournament in Memphis by playing with the type of reckless abandon that's more like the way Lanny played. Did I learn this lesson too late? Would playing more of a Lanny Wadkins style of golf have put me into the winner's circle more often? Well, we'll never know. What I do know is that Lanny and I don't always agree when we analyze a golf tournament, but it livens up the broadcast and hopefully makes things more interesting for our viewers.

I'm very confident that every contestant in every tournament is trying his heart out to play the best he can play. Golf, however, is a fickle game. The ground isn't always level. The ball doesn't always bounce straight, and Lady Luck isn't always on your side. I try to keep these thoughts in mind as I go through a broadcast. I

Interviewing Dana Quigley and Tom Watson

also try to keep in mind Theodore Roosevelt's famous admonition that "It's not the critic that counts . . . the credit belongs to the man who is actually inside the arena." I have the entire "Man in the Arena" quote framed on my desk and have for decades, as a reminder of what President Theodore Roosevelt so eloquently expressed as his view of a critic. I totally agree with his assessment, and try to keep that perspective when broadcasting a golf tournament.

The greatest thing about pro golf, there's no end to it unless you're dead. You just go from here to the Senior Tour.

—FUZZY ZOELLER

CHAPTER 10

PHYSICAL ISSUES

A number of physical issues began to surface toward the end of my career on the Champions Tour, and they really compromised my ability to hit the type of golf shot that was acceptable to me.

At first I thought these physical things were the result of countless hours spent pounding golf balls, and I blamed my recurring back and hip problems on practicing too much. The strange thing is, I'd always had above-average flexibility and had worked hard for years to maintain it. So it didn't make sense that I was experiencing this level of pain.

Earlier in my career, Steve Carlton, the Hall of Fame pitcher, referred me to a video produced by Gus Hoefling, who was the conditioning coach for the Philadelphia Phillies. Gus developed an innovative fitness program based on martial arts skills that emphasized flexibility and strength. I religiously followed Gus's program for many years. Later on I met Adrian Crook, a firefighter in California who trained a number of prominent athletes—notably Nomar Garciaparra, an All-Star shortstop for the Boston Red Sox, and Karch Kiraly, an Olympic gold medal winner in volleyball. Adrian introduced more yoga into his program, and that provided even greater flexibility.

I can't emphasize the importance of a sound conditioning program for any golfer. The reason professional careers are lasting longer and 50- and 60-year-olds are still competing at the highest levels is the new focus on conditioning. When I first came on the Tour in the early '70s, few if any golfers did any type of exercise other than hitting golf balls. Now many players have their own personal trainer who travels with them. The most popular after-round gathering point has moved from the hotel bar to the fitness trailer.

This emphasis on fitness should also extend to the amateur golfer. A sound program that works on strength, flexibility, and balance will help to improve any level of golfer. I believe the stretching programs I used helped me to have more longevity in playing.

When it got to the point that the pain became unbearable, I finally went to see a doctor. His examination revealed that most of my physical problems were related to my hips. As I'd been born prematurely, my hips hadn't had a chance to fully develop. Because of this malformation in the hips, my body was compensating in other areas during the golf swing, eventually causing spasms and pain in my back and legs. It was actually a relief to learn that a bilateral hip replacement would soon become my only option and that the operation should relieve the pain. I didn't, however, run out right away and schedule the surgery. Facing such a major operation was scary, and I decided to wait a while, maybe secretly hoping things would improve.

> "You walk like you're a hundred years old."
> —Peter Jacobsen

Time for Surgery

At the Legends of Golf in April 2010, Peter Jacobsen approached me and asked how my hips were working. I said fine and he laughed at me. Then he said, "I don't think so. You walk like you're a hundred years old."

Peter suggested I do myself a favor and call the doctor who had performed his hip surgery. Mort Bertram is a fine surgeon and also a plus-2 handicap golfer who played on the golf team with Russ Cochran at the University of Kentucky. Peter insisted Dr. Bertram really knew what he was doing and had performed the same surgery on Johnny Bench. I first called Johnny Bench, who highly recommended Dr. Bertram. The next step was to call to Dr. Bertram in Florida.

Not long after that, I traveled to Naples to take care of all the initial examinations and pre-op testing. This process took about three days and when they had finished, they called me into the office to present the results. The doctor who coordinated all the testing was a woman who believed in being very thorough. X-rays, blood tests, CT scans, and heart monitor exams were all part of her workup.

She told me she was concerned about two things. One was the condition of my heart, and the other was the fact that she thought I might have lung cancer. At that time I was a heavy smoker, and the tests revealed a high percentage of nicotine in my blood. She sent me out to have more tests run, with the assurance that she would have the results the next day.

I was scared to death and didn't sleep much that night. When I got the call from her at noon the next day, I was afraid to answer the phone. She said, "Mr. Mahaffey, you're a lucky man. You have nothing wrong with your heart and you have no cancer. You have a second chance, so what are you going to do about your smoking?"

I put the smokes down that day in late April of 2010 and haven't had one since. That in itself is pretty remarkable, as anyone who has ever known me knows how hooked I was on cigarettes. To compound things, my father died from lung cancer, pretty much as a result of his cigarette smoking. I always knew I should quit, and I tried many times to do so. Over the years, I've tried every device, therapy, and voodoo chant to try to break the miserable habit. I even went as far as wearing earrings that were supposed to be a "can't miss" acupuncture technique, but none of these methods had the lasting effect of getting a reprieve from a lung cancer diagnosis.

Dr. Bertram was especially pleased that I decided to quit because smokers take longer to heal from operations, so rehab would take less time now that I'd quit. I was looking forward to new hips and a longer, smoke-free life.

> If not for my bilateral hip replacement, I would have ended up in a wheelchair.

A Surgeon with a +3 Handicap

Three months later, in July of 2010, I returned to Naples, Florida, and had a bilateral hip replacement. Afterward, Dr. Bertram told me I had the worst hips he had ever seen or operated on. If I'd not had the surgery when I did, I would have ended up in a wheelchair all too soon. I had the surgery not specifically to play golf but to have a better quality of life without pain. Thanks to Dr. Bertram I do have a great quality of life that is indeed pain-free.

By the way, I've also had the opportunity to play golf with Mort, and if he were to decide to give up his day job, I believe he would do quite well on the Champions Tour. I know he would be in the top five in driving distance. He hits it forever and has a beautiful golf swing to go along with it. Mort loves the game of golf and is always looking for ways to improve.

During my recovery period, I was staying at a Residence Inn in Naples. He would stop by regularly to check on the progress of my hips, which usually took him about two minutes. Then for the next 45 minutes, he would show me photos of his practice session taken that morning when he was hitting golf balls, wanting my comments. I'll always wonder—were his visits about the hips, or were they about the golf? Good question!

CHAPTER 11

PRESENT DAY—RANDOM THOUGHTS

One great thing golf has taught me is the necessity to be self-reliant. In golf, it's you alone who must make the final decision before hitting a shot. You alone must commit to the execution of that shot and take responsibility for the result. There are no teammates to blame for a mistake. It's all on you, win or lose. Golf makes you focus and become more aware of what's going on around you. These things also carry over to life off the golf course. In anything you do, when you're more aware of your

With Brian Hammons on the Golf Channel set, during the final round of the 2014 Nature Valley First Tee Open

surroundings, you can make more intelligent decisions. These decisions are what mold you and determine your quality of life. We pay the price for poor decisions and are rewarded for wise ones.

It's no surprise that many great golfers are also successful in off-course ventures. That self-reliant attitude breeds a level of confidence that works quite well in business, and Arnold Palmer is its poster boy.

That same self-reliance that carried Palmer from the fairways of Latrobe to the pinnacle of the world of golf also helped him to become a corporate dynamo. His life story is Horatio Alger on steroids. Ben Hogan and Jack Nicklaus are other examples of this type of crossover success.

But would any of these guys have been as successful in business if it weren't for their golfing success? My feeling is: absolutely. Maybe not to the extent that they achieved, as being a household name would certainly help any startup business. But the self-reliance that enabled them to excel on the fairways is not something that can be taught. It needs to be part of a person's DNA. Whether it's further developed on the fairway or in the boardroom doesn't matter. A self-reliant person will always be a winner.

A self-reliant person will always be a winner.

As I reflect back on over 50 years of banging golf balls, I realize that I was so lucky to be able to play in the era I did. When I played in my first professional tournament, the 1970 US Open, the total prize money for the entire year was $6.7 million. Now that amount is an average purse size for a single tournament. The growth of golf has also had an enormous effect on charities. The PGA Tour estimates it's raised over $2 billion for charities over the years. This is just the tip of the iceberg. Virtually any day around the country, there's a charity golf event raising money for something. Whether the cause is buying a new X-ray machine for a local hospital, sending a high school band to the Rose Bowl Parade, or helping the family of a soldier wounded in battle, a golf tournament is the perfect vehicle. It would be interesting to count up all the dollars golf actually raises in a given year.

Looking forward, the future of golf is standing at a precipice. On one hand, there's more money in the sport than ever before. Equipment is better and scores are lower. On the other hand, more golf courses are closing than are being built.

We're trying to develop future generations of golfers through programs like The First Tee, Kids Golf 4 Free, and others. These not only promote the game of golf but also teach youngsters the life skills necessary to become proactive and productive citizens. Learning the values and work ethic that permeate the game will enable these youngsters to be leaders in whatever field they choose and set the example for others to follow.

Over the years, golf courses have been venues where a lot of business is discussed in a beautiful, relaxed atmosphere. Playing a round of golf with people is also a great way to size them up by observing how they play the game. It's not just how well they score, but it's seeing if they play by the rules or skirt around them. That performance can give you a good idea of someone's character. The junior programs emphasize the importance of character at a most important time in a child's development.

My concern is whether or not these young men and women will either have a place to play or will be able to afford to play when they grow up. Golf is one of the few sports that can be enjoyed for a lifetime. It's a wonderful way for a family to spend time together outdoors. I was fortunate to grow up on a public course. That was the only way I was able to play, because it was affordable for my parents. I understand golf has become big business, but I hope we don't price ourselves out of the market and deprive future potential major champions of even getting the chance to experience the game.

In today's world, a day of golf at some of the nice resorts can run close to $500 per person and up, when you include greens fees, carts or caddies, and meals. This is at the high end of the scale. Most places in this price range are very special in either their location or unique design, and they can demand high prices. They are destination venues that golfers dream of playing, if only just once.

> Self-examination can be cathartic and expose the things that keep us from achieving our dreams.

What we need most are golf courses for people who have completed or outgrown the youth programs so they can continue to play, and affordable places for adults just getting started. Perhaps if more people could play golf in this new world of instant gratification, those same people could take a brief holiday from their hectic life and spend some time getting acquainted with the beauty of nature. It might also give them a chance for some self-examination, which is always a good idea.

Self-examination can be cathartic and expose the poisonous things that keep us from achieving our dreams. We all have regrets, things we wish we could change if we could go back in time. Of course that's not possible, but we can learn from those past mistakes. Looking back, one of my biggest regrets is that I allowed off-course, outside factors to interfere with my loftiest goals. When I became more interested in the nightlife than the day life, my career suffered. I advise anyone truly dedicated to the pursuit of greatness in their chosen field to keep their head firmly wrapped around their final objective. Refrain from getting caught up in things that can jeopardize what you work so hard to achieve. Don't throw it all away for a life empty of substance.

Revelation

During my early adult life, I developed a great fondness for alcohol. Over time, it got to the point that I couldn't control it and it took control of me. It affected my friendships, my personal relationships, and my ability to play the game I loved so much. While I was under the influence, I said and did hurtful things to people I cared about, things I wish I could take back. Alcohol took precedence over everything in my life. I was oblivious to the fact that things were crumbling all around me, until a very close acquaintance asked me a pointed question one spring morning.

"God, you have got to help me because we both know I can't do this alone."

It was May 16, 2000, at 10:00 in the morning in Wichita, Kansas. I was staying in the pool house at the home of my good friend Tom Devlin, an entrepreneur who possessed the same passion for golf that I did. After a particularly rough night, I'd already popped open a beer when he walked into my room. He looked at me, then at the beer in my hand, and shook his head. Then he asked me the question that would change my life forever. He started by saying, "It's really none of my business and we'll still be friends if you don't want to answer this, but I have to ask it. Could everything bad that is now happening or has happened in your life be related to your abuse of alcohol?" That question stopped me dead in my tracks, and for a moment I was speechless, because I knew the answer was yes.

I didn't answer him directly, but I asked if he could get me on a flight back to Houston that afternoon. He knew he had hit home, and he made the reservation. My plan was to first get to my home in The Woodlands. I needed to be alone because I had some serious thinking to do. I poured the beer down the drain and got busy packing.

When I got home, I still wasn't sure how I was going to address my alcohol problem, since I'd tried so many times in the past. Some of my efforts had lasted for a month or so, but I always found an excuse to fall off the wagon. I thought hard, got down on my knees, looked up to the sky, and said, "God, you have got to help me because we both know I can't do this alone." I came from a Christian upbringing, but until that moment I never understood the power of prayer. It seemed to work, as something that I could never defeat in the past now became something that I no longer cared about. My last drink was that half beer at Tom Devlin's in Wichita in 2000. The withdrawal was painful and very real. The memory of that process is a constant reminder that I never again want anything to have that kind of control over me. Over time my true friends came back and I was fortunate to make new ones. That, in itself, is a great feeling, coupled with the knowledge that I'd eliminated the biggest negative in my life.

As much as I knew that achievement required commitment, sacrifice, and a burning desire, and as much as I thought I had each of those qualities, I found there were others who were willing to give more. Experience has taught me that some people get caught up in the

> It's easy to say everything was worth it when you're holding up the trophy on a Sunday afternoon.

moment, while others seize that moment and shine. I had my chance and now understand that I turned a realistic Hall of Fame career into something much less. My father always talked to me about choices. Mr. Hogan talked to me about choices. If only I'd listened more closely. If only I'd paid attention. If only I'd really believed, I could have made better choices. I will always regret I didn't make those better choices.

Was it worth it? That's the question we all ask ourselves when we're faced with the consequences of a particular course of action. In reality the question should be, *is it worth it?* It would be much wiser to ask the question in real time, when you're actually facing one of those difficult choices, rather than asking yourself, *was it worth it?* after the fact.

It's easy to say everything was worth it when you're holding up the trophy on a Sunday afternoon. Even if you'd made some bad decisions along the way, they get obscured temporarily by the moment in the sun. Instead, the focus should be on the close calls, when you could've won but came up just short. Here's where self-examination should come into play. Was it worth it to stay out and party? It's easy to play the "What if?" game, but I wish I'd had the opportunity to go back and change those *Was it worth it?* times to *Is it worth it?* choices. A person only gets so many opportunities to grab that brass ring; there isn't an endless number of chances. You don't really understand this until you get older and those endless chances become fewer and fewer. It's all about priorities and what's most important to you.

> Getting back to that, *"was it worth it"* question, for me the answer is a resounding *Yes!*

That being said, what's truly amazing to me is that as my physical inability to perform began to take away the enjoyment of playing golf, my fondness for the game actually grew because of television. Broadcasting opened a new chapter in my life and has allowed me to continue to use my knowledge gained through experience, my expertise learned through trial and error, and my ability to tell a few stories to help keep a bit of the history of the game alive. The best part is, more history is being made every day and I get see a lot of it as it happens.

As I reflect back on the years that have passed since that day in 1959 when I first picked up a golf club, it's amazing to me how much the world has changed. We've evolved from the party line telephones back in Kerrville to Skype calls with people around the world. Since 1959, we've gone through 13 presidents and several wars. The Berlin Wall went up and came down. We've put men on the moon and women in the boardroom. Each new day, the world spins faster and seems to get smaller.

The one thing that's pretty much remained constant over the years is the game of golf. Sure the equipment is different today than it was in 1959, but the game itself is basically unchanged. Guys battling it out each Sunday, whether on the PGA Tour or on their local golf course, are much the same as they were during the '50s. The names are different but the game is the same. Golf is still the true American Dream. The person who performs the best makes the most.

Getting back to that *Was it worth it?* question, for me the answer is a resounding *Yes!* It's been worth every moment. It's been my privilege to be a small part of the game and to have had the opportunity to compete on golf's biggest stages. From that moment back in Kerrville in 1961, when I made that imaginary putt to win my 53rd major championship up to today, I've been one of the most fortunate human beings on earth. Not only have I had the opportunity to live my dream, but I've also had the chance to evolve under the watchful eye of Ben Hogan, one of the greatest players and human beings who ever lived.

I hope this glimpse into my journey in the world of competitive golf has been entertaining and informative from a historical perspective. As the game continues to grow globally, I hope you're looking forward to witnessing more extraordinary feats from today's players as much as I am. Professional golfers never cease to amaze. The depth of their talent and imagination assures me that the evolution of the game is in very capable hands. Be assured, I'll be watching.

*If there's a golf course
in heaven, I hope it's like
Augusta National. I just don't
want an early tee time.*

—GARY PLAYER

INDEX

*But in the end it's still
a game of golf, and if at the
end of the day you can't shake
hands with your opponents and
still be friends, then you've
missed the point.*

—PAYNE STEWART

PHOTO CREDITS

The following illustrations are included with permission.

Cover Photo
Bill Knight, sports photographer

Front Flap
AP Images

Back Cover
Mahaffey Family Archives

Preface
Jimmy Demaret, Ben Hogan, Sam Snead and Jackie Burke at the Palm Beach Round Robin, 1950. AP Images

Chapter 1
My dad receiving the Bronze Star during World War II. Mahaffey Family Archives

My father during World War II. Mahaffey Family Archives

My mother and father, John and Eloise Mahaffey. Mahaffey Family Archives

High School graduation. Mahaffey Family Archives

Chapter 2
Dave Williams, Univ. of Houston Golf Team Coach (1951–1985). Mahaffey Family Archives

Proud member of the U of H Golf Team. Mahaffey Family Archives

Chapter 3

Jackie Burke winning the 1961 Flint Open. AP Images

Ben Hogan and Jimmy Demaret, 1940 Masters. AP Images

Chapter 4

Perfection by Ben Hogan. AP Images

Chapter 6

J.C, Snead, Sam Snead, and me in Miami Springs, 2002. Terry Ferrero

My first Tour win at the 1973 Sahara Invitational in Las Vegas. AP Images

Lee Trevino, Arnold Palmer, and me, 2006 Administaff Small Business Classic. AP Images

Lou Graham and me at the 1975 US Open. AP Images

Winning the 1978 PGA Championship. AP Images

Me and my mother at John Mahaffey Appreciation Day in Kerrville. Mahaffey Family Archives

Warming up with Byron Nelson. Mahaffey Family Archives

The 1979 Ryder Cup US Team. Getty Images

Receiving a diamond ring from Ben Hogan. Mahaffey Family Archives

Me and Billy Ray Brown. Mahaffey Family Archives

Chapter 7

Winning the Anheuser-Busch Golf Classic. AP Images

Winning the Players Championship in 1986. Getty Images

Chapter 8

Practice, practice, practice. AP Images

Chapter 9

Hogan's beautiful swing. AP Images

Interviewing the immortal Seve Ballesteros. Getty Images

With Lanny Wadkins on the Golf Channel set. Mahaffey Family Archives

Dave Marr flanked by his sons Tony and David III, my colleague on the Golf Channel. David Marr III

Interviewing Dana Quigley and Tom Watson. Getty Images

Chapter 11

Me and Brian Hammond on the Golf Channel set. Golf Channel

If you watch a game, it's fun.
If you play it, it's recreation.
If you work at it, it's golf.

—BOB HOPE

ABOUT THE AUTHORS

JOHN MAHAFFEY

John Mahaffey is a professional golfer on the PGA Tour. Between 1973 and 1999, he won ten events on the PGA Tour, including the 1978 PGA Championship and the 1986 Players Championship. His last PGA win was on the Champions Tour, at the 1999 Southwestern Bell Dominion.

A native of Kerrville, Texas, John is a graduate of the University of Houston, where he became part of the NCAA golf powerhouse created by legendary coach Dave Williams. In addition to being a member of two NCAA national championship teams, John was a two-time first-team All American, as well as the 1970 NCAA individual champion. He graduated in 1970 with a degree in psychology.

Following graduation, John tied for low amateur with Ben Crenshaw in the 1970 US Open at Hazeltine National Golf Club in Chaska, Minnesota, and turned pro in 1971.

Two of John's most exciting years on the PGA tour were 1978 and 1979. In 1978 he won back-to-back tour events: the PGA Championship followed by the American Optical Championship. He also won the World Cup individual that year, plus the team event paired with Andy North at Princeville on the Hawaiian island of Kauai. John played on the victorious 1979 Ryder Cup team and the World Cup team that same year in Athens, Greece, with Hale Irvin as his partner.

In 2003, John was successful in making the challenging transition from pro golfer to announcer/analyst on Golf Channel covering the Champions Tour.

Off the course John released his first book *Hogan's Boy: A Journey In Golf*, plus he hosts a monthly radio show called *A Glimpse of Greatness*, on Sirius 208 XM 93 PGA Tour Radio. John also delivers motivational keynote speeches filled with great stories about golf and life.

John currently lives in The Woodlands, Texas, with his wife Elizabeth. He has a son, J.D., and daughter, Meagan.

In his spare time John enjoys fishing and writing, and he always enjoys promoting the game of golf.

JOHN CADEN

John Caden is a graduate of the University of Connecticut. He is an entrepreneur who established several highly successful businesses in the health care field.

He recently retired, and along with his wife Linda, he moved to Ponte Vedra Beach, Florida, to reacquaint himself with the game of golf near the home of the PGA Tour.

He has been a good friend of John Mahaffey's since the early 1970s. He persuaded Mahaffey to complete a book he had been struggling with for almost a decade, offering to help in any way he could.

It was John Caden's idea to use as the title of this book the moniker that Sam Snead gave to Mahaffey at their first meeting—*Hogan's Boy.*

Hogan's Boy
A journey in golf

Hogan's Boy is available at special discounts for bulk purchases. Let us show you creative ways to use John's book to help you acquire new customers and strengthen existing customer goodwill with autographs, customized covers, and inserts.

For book information, contact Davonna Blasingame at dblas@sbnbooks.com.

For speeches, appearances, and outings with John Mahaffey, contact Elizabeth at HogansBoy@comcast.net.

For more information, including where to buy Hogan's Boy in hard cover or e-book, go to HogansBoy.com.